Roberto Pasini • Remo Schiavo

THE VERONA ARENA
THE LARGEST OPERA HOUSE IN THE WORLD

Photographs by
Gianfranco Fainello

arsenale editrice

Roberto Pasini • Remo Schiavo
THE VERONA ARENA
THE LARGEST OPERA HOUSE IN THE WORLD

Photographs by
Gianfranco Fainello

Translation
Conor O'Malley

Printed in Italy by
EBS Editoriale Bortolazzi-Stei, Verona

First edition
July 1995
Arsenale Editrice srl
San Polo 1789
I – 30125 Venice

ISBN 88-7743-154-7

CONTENTS

THE ARENA
AND ITS HISTORY

Roberto Pasini

THE ARENA AND VERONA

Almost everything about the Arena poses questions: a monument of such vast bulk, such uncertain style and such varied uses intrigues not merely the occasional visitor but also those who regularly attend performances there and even the citizens of Verona, whose prime perception of the Arena is as a picturesque backdrop to their city's largest square.

The sheer size of the Arena immediately prompts one to wonder why the Romans built it to hold so many spectators. How was such a feat possible with the construction technologies then available? Who conceived, designed and implemented the immense project? And stylistic questions are no easier to answer. As it stands, the Arena is a hugely impressive ruin, apparently just a mass of building materials almost entirely lacking in the distinctive features that architecture normally confers on the finished form rather than its structural core: the shape, size and decorative detail with which the architect balances doors, windows, walls and roofing to give a building character, harmony and visible style. And over the years of course, the Arena, like most ancient buildings, has been altered and restored many times, thus making it still less easy to imagine what it was originally like; even the specialist historians with their archive documents and comparative studies sometimes fail to agree on fundamental points. And as for what the Arena is for, the tens of thousands of people who enter its gates every year do so for an astonishingly wide range of reasons ranging from papal visits to operas, rock concerts, Cup football matches, trade union rallies, religious festivals, veteran soldiers' reunions ..., for the Arena is and has always been a venue for mass meetings of all kinds more than just for entertainment; a gathering place for special occasions which are usually festive and celebratory in character but by no means always.

Obviously the questions we continue to ask now have all been asked a thousand times in the past. But often the answers put forward have enhanced the "mystery" of the Arena rather than dispel the uncertainties, surrounding the place with legends to complement those of the star-crossed lovers, Romeo and Juliet, and Verona's iniquitous ruler Theodoric, and weaving the magic mantle with which the city enfolds first-time visitors just as it stops those born and bred there from ever really leaving.

In attempting our own answer to the "question" of the Arena therefore, we must approach its complexity in an orderly fashion and insist at all costs on avoiding legend.

Aerial view of the Arena with Piazza Bra and the centre of Verona.

First of all, time and place: the specific site chosen for the construction of the amphitheatre during the growth of the Roman town.

Verona existed as a place of intersection between various territories and peoples – the Veneti, the Gauls and the Raetians – long before Rome conquered Cisalpine Gaul in the II Cent. B.C., but it was completely refounded as a Roman *municipium* during and after the time of Julius Caesar, from the middle of the I Cent. B.C. on. As the meeting point between a great waterway (the River Adige) and the most important land routes from the Tyrrhenian to the Adriatic (the Via Postumia), from the Apennines to the Alps (the Via Claudia Augusta) and along the line of the foothills of the Alps at the northern edge of the plain of the Po (the Via Gallica), Verona was the natural focal point for traffic and trade between the urban and rural centres of a very extensive area. The impressive and efficient road system created by the Romans, and the freedom and safety enjoyed by merchants in the Roman social and economic world further enhanced this central position.

And the city also stands at a point where the coils of the Adige seem to be holding together mountains and plains, making it a meeting point for upland and lowland economies and an ideal place for social and commercial interchange for peoples of different cultures and interests. In the centralist and interethnic vision of Roman policy and administration, any potential a place might have for economic and cultural integration was enthusiastically encouraged. And one of the main forms this encouragement took was the building of a large amphitheatre: indeed, the presence of an amphitheatre in a Roman city reveals, or confirms, the "pivotal" position of the city and its ability regularly to attract vast numbers of people.

Above, a late-mediaeval engraving depicting the city as "Madonna Verona".

Right, the layout of Verona in Roman times, with the Arena outside the defensive walls and the Roman theatre on the other side of the River Adige.

Opposite, a plan of the Roman amphitheatre.

Conversely, the amphitheatre represented a sort of "metropolitan" service aimed at users in a territory that was considerably vaster than the urban area and its immediate rural hinterland.

Before we examine the nature of the service provided, let us stop to observe how the Romans built the Arena outside their city walls, suggesting that the amphitheatre was not intended only for the city in the same way as urban services such as baths, the theatre, the basilica or temples were; rather it stood beside the city as a kind of adjunct, with the implication that it was also to be used by a wider public. This explains why a city calculated to have about ten thousand inhabitants should have an amphitheatre capable

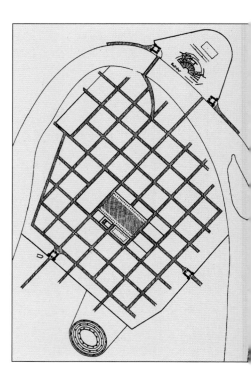

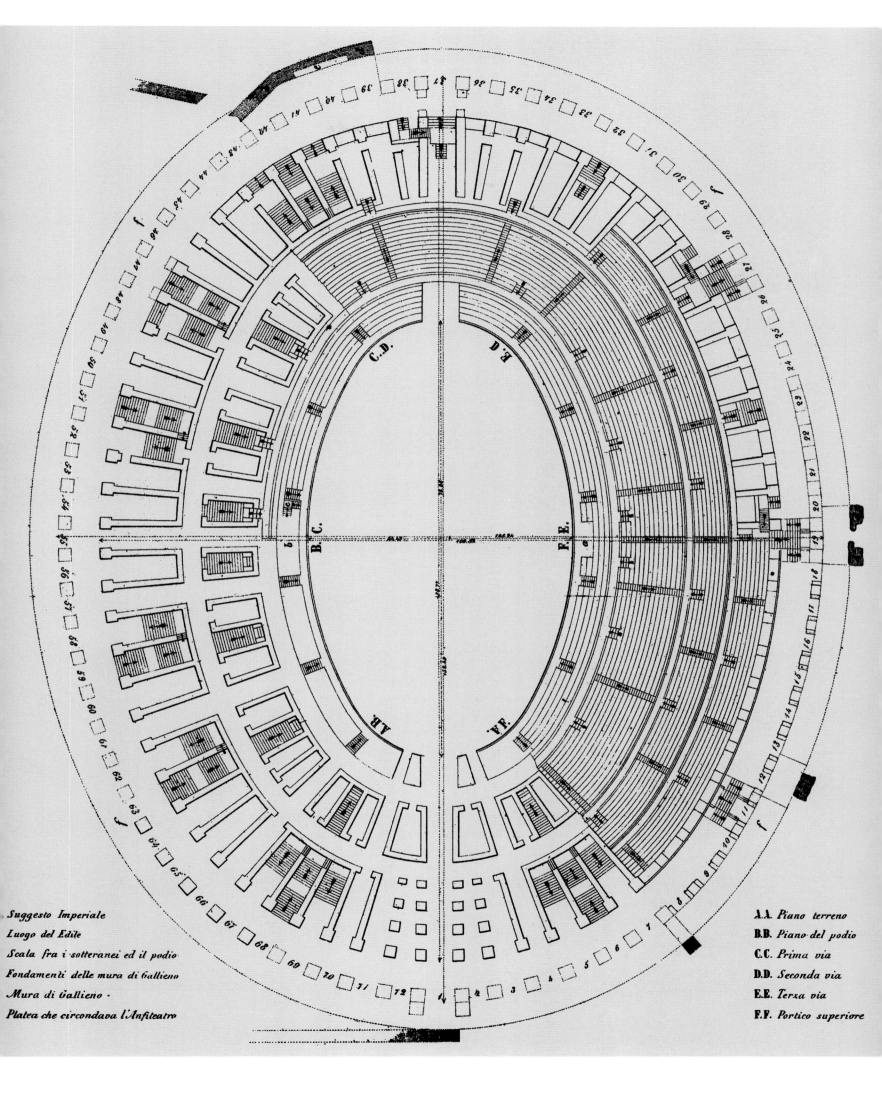

Suggesto Imperiale

Luogo del Edile

Scala fra i sotteranei ed il podio

Fondamenti delle mura di Gallieno

Mura di Gallieno ·

Platea che circondava l'Anfiteatro

A.A. *Piano terreno*

B.B. *Piano del podio*

C.C. *Prima via*

D.D. *Seconda via*

E.E. *Terza via*

F.F. *Portico superiore*

Details of modern elevation and section drawings of the external ring of the Arena.

of holding almost three times that number.

The right-angle corner of the walls of the original Roman *castrum* was about eighty metres from the Arena, one wall running from the Adige as far as the present-day via Leoncino in line with Porta Borsari, and the other going from the Adige along via Leoncino in line with Porta Leoni. It was only later that the walls were extended to include the Arena, when the Emperor Gallienus decided that the fortifications of Verona should be overhauled in response to the threat of the first incursions of the Germanic tribes. So in 265 A.D. the Arena was, as it were, gathered into the city and lost, at least in part, its symbolic and real functions (at much the same time there was a certain decline in the popularity of gladiatorial contests).

This moment in the Arena's history marks a turning point in the life and physical shape of Verona, and poses a new series of questions. Why did the amphitheatre have to be incorporated into the city? Were the new walls built around the Arena or did they merge directly into the outer wall of the Arena itself? Still more intriguing is the question of whether the Arena's outer wall, the so-called *ala*, was completely in place before 265 A.D. or whether the materials assembled to build it were used instead to extend the city walls. And if this was the case, to which period or periods in the development of the Roman city can we attribute the building of the amphitheatre?

Authoritative answers to these questions would seem to have been provided by the excavations carried out in the late 1800s. These showed that the new wall built at the command of Gallienus stood at a distance of about five metres from the outer wall of the Arena, and that the foundations of the *ala* existed right round the perimeter. So in all probability the outer wall was constructed at the same time as the rest of the amphitheatre.

No written document, historical account or inscription survives to tell us with certainty when the Arena was built. There is a letter by Pliny the Younger that confirms that the amphitheatre was being used in his day, but he was a contemporary of Trajan and lived at the end of the I and beginning of the II Cent. A.D.. So 49 B.C., when the Romans refounded Verona, and Pliny's letter a century and a half later give us the earliest and latest possible dates. The once widely held opinion that it was built at the same time as the Colosseum, during the period of the Flavian Emperors (69-98 A.D.) has now been discounted, and authoritative opinion is currently in favour of a dating

during the second or third decades of the I Cent. A.D..
We can therefore conclude that when Verona was refounded
by the Romans in the late Republican period, there were no
plans to build an amphitheatre. Later, when it was decided
the city needed one, it had to be put outside the walls
because most of the space inside was used up already or
designated for development. It seems extremely improbable
that it was always intended to stand outside the walls: in that
position it is higher than the walls and would almost
certainly have weakened the defensive system; it might have
served as a fortified outpost outside the city, but equally, if
the enemy gained control of it it could have become a
powerful base from which to conduct a siege. In actual fact,
as soon as a danger appeared the authorities hastened to
enlarge the city so as to incorporate it within the walls. This
must also mean that the amphitheatre was built during a
period of peace and security, a fact that further supports the
assumption that the Arena was at least started during the
Augustan period.

But even more convincing evidence lies in the sober style of
what few decorative features survive on the short length of
the outer *ala* wall, a style which was typical of the late
Republican period and which was still found in the
provinces during the early Empire. And finally, comparison
with contemporary or almost contemporary amphitheatres in
relatively close provinces such as Pula and Aosta, and with
those of Nîmes and Arles in Gallia Narbonensis provides
yet more corroboration of the suggested dating.

The Arena in Verona is bigger than any of these, however;
indeed it is only slightly smaller than the largest of all
Roman amphitheatres, the Colosseum in Rome itself. Which
leads us to the question of who built the Arena, and how.
The building typology of the amphitheatre is specifically
Roman, so we can be quite certain that the Arena too was
conceived in Rome. But the Romans must have held their
architects in rather low esteem for inscriptions almost never
mention their names beside those of the magistrates
responsible for public works and the rich patricians who
paid for them. In the case of the Arena, we do not even
know the names of the benefactors, still less those of the
architects, though various records of other generous gifts to
the city have survived, such as the matron Massima Gavia's
bequest of half a million sesterces for the aqueduct. Then
again, it is quite possible that the building of the Arena was
not supervised by a single architect but was rather the work
of a team of experienced master-builders. In actual fact,

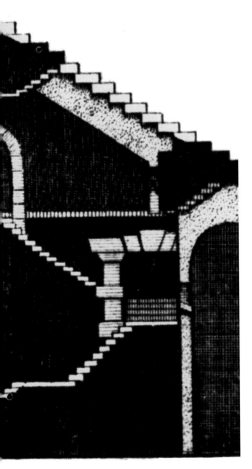

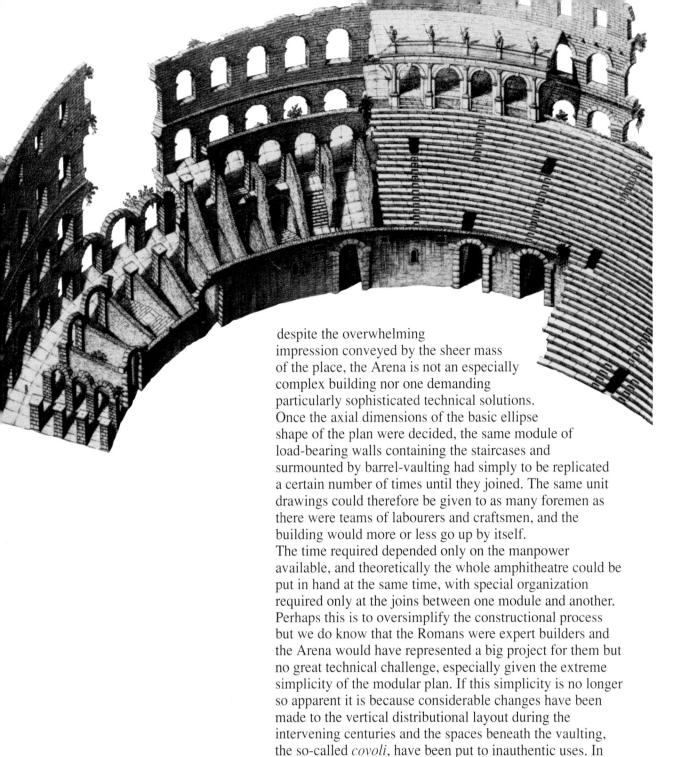

despite the overwhelming
impression conveyed by the sheer mass
of the place, the Arena is not an especially
complex building nor one demanding
particularly sophisticated technical solutions.
Once the axial dimensions of the basic ellipse
shape of the plan were decided, the same module of
load-bearing walls containing the staircases and
surmounted by barrel-vaulting had simply to be replicated
a certain number of times until they joined. The same unit
drawings could therefore be given to as many foremen as
there were teams of labourers and craftsmen, and the
building would more or less go up by itself.
The time required depended only on the manpower
available, and theoretically the whole amphitheatre could be
put in hand at the same time, with special organization
required only at the joins between one module and another.
Perhaps this is to oversimplify the constructional process
but we do know that the Romans were expert builders and
the Arena would have represented a big project for them but
no great technical challenge, especially given the extreme
simplicity of the modular plan. If this simplicity is no longer
so apparent it is because considerable changes have been
made to the vertical distributional layout during the
intervening centuries and the spaces beneath the vaulting,
the so-called *covoli*, have been put to inauthentic uses. In
brief, none of the staircases in use today is consistent with
the original plan, the banked terraces of the amphitheatre
were extensively rebuilt during the Renaissance, when the
two rostrums were also inserted, and there remain several
eye-confusing examples of voids arbritrarily filled in during
the Middle Ages.
Another element that must considerably have simplified
matters for the builders and at the same time ensured that
the modules constructed by the various teams of workmen

Enlarged details of two engravings of the Arena made in the first half of the 1700s by Francesco Masieri, then "custodian" of the amphitheatre.

actually fitted together in the end was the initial choice of a basic relationship linking the dimensions of every individual part, so that every measurement was proportionate to another. Thus the two axes of the ellipse forming the Arena measure 75.68 and 44.43 metres, which convert into Roman feet at the significantly round figures of 250 and 150 and establish the basic ratio of 5/3. For the thoroughly practical and realistic Romans the decision to work to such proportional measurements derived less from a desire to achieve aesthetic harmony than from the recognition that it provided an easy way of ensuring effective coordination of all building operations. The system reduced unforseen contingencies to a minimum and enabled all the materials to be prepared beforehand – stone could safely be shaped and dressed at the quarry, for example – and brought to the site ready for assembly.

As well as being modular, the Arena's constructional design is particularly solid. The load-bearing structure all dovetails together: the inner three elliptical, barrel-vaulted galleries all fit into the cross-walls radiating from the circumference of the ellipse; and the external gallery, the one that ran between what is now the outer wall and the *ala*, was at two superimposed levels.

However, there is no disguising the huge efforts both men and animals must have made to raise the immense structure. So much is obvious from the size of the blocks of stone they had to lift up to thirty metres from the ground and the even heavier masses that comprise the tiers of seats banked around the arena itself.

Almost everything in the actual fabric of the amphitheatre is made of stone, except for the vaulting which was a mixture, *in opus incertum*, of pebbles and concrete.

And the foundations? Rather than single foundations the Arena rests on a vast, solid and completely stable bed of concrete covering the whole area. The concrete layer is furrowed by drainage conduits that funnelled rainwater into the sewerage system that followed the three elliptical galleries and in turn emptied into the main drains laid along the axes of the ellipse, which probably led ultimately to the Adige or its tributaries. The constructional technique used is the same as that adopted for the sewers beneath the Roman

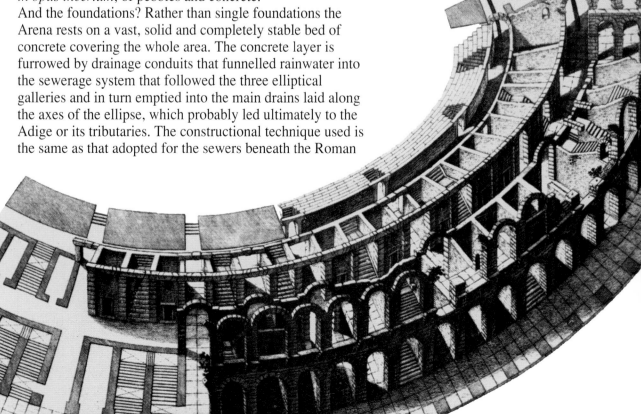

Below, a detail of the "ala" or external wall of the Arena, from a French aquatint of 1830.

city's streets, further confirmation of the suggested dating for the Arena.

The question that now presents itself concerns the provenance of the enormous quantity of stone the builders used. It is easy to recognise the type – it is obviously limestone from the Lessini Mountains – but where exactly did it come from?

The stone was certainly brought to the city by water so it must have been quarried somewhere along the Adige near the beginning of the valley where there are still working quarries to this day. An interesting but unsupported theory is that removal of the stone for the Arena resulted in the formation of the narrow Chiusa gorge and the consequent drainage of the supposedly marshy Vallagarina (the name contains a convenient echo of "Arena") immediately to the north of the Chiusa gorge. Knowing the superb engineering capacities of the Romans and their achievements in draining bogs in many parts of the Empire, the theory is an attractive one, but for it to be credible one would surely expect human intervention on such a massive scale to have left some trace on the natural landscape. An appealing aspect of the theory is the image it offers of the dismantling of a mountain, piece by piece, and its reassembly far away at the gates of the city. But though the Arena retained a mountainous massiveness, it also acquired its architectural character in the move. The magnificent construction features clear connections between its underlying skeleton, the tiered seats around the arena and the exterior of the outer wall, i.e. between the structure, its function and its decoration. Above the three concentric galleries surrounding the arena ran three corridors (the upper one no longer exists) dividing the tiered seating into three orders, whereas the position of the staircases that divide the seating into wedge-shaped sectors corresponds to the cross-walls radiating from the circumference of the arena. The three orders of arches comprising the outer wall (the *ala*) reflect the three orders of seating inside, the arches themselves correspond to vaulting towards the interior and the walls supporting the vaulting are marked by the pilasters and pilaster strips in the outer wall. This convergence of the ideals of solidity, functional efficiency and formal order (*firmitas, utilitas,* and *venustas*) makes the Arena one of the finest examples of the Roman conception of public architecture.

Now we can imagine all the severe elegance of the monument as it orginally stood. When it surrounded it completely, the *ala* must have made it look much taller; the

Detail of a mosaic depicting Roman gladiators, excavated in the Roman part of the city. Verona, Archaeological Museum.

triple order of arches which diminish in height as they rise will also have enhanced this apparent upward thrust. Inside, the top corridor ran beneath a column-supported loggia, which must have looked like a deep and shady encircling crown above the bare expanse of tiered seating sloping away below. There seems also to have been some form of awning that could be extended over a trellis of ropes to shade spectators from the sun.

Down in the arena we can imagine the gladiatorial contests, the competitions between armed men and the baiting and hunting down of fierce wild animals that aroused the enthusiasms of Romans of all ages and social classes and of both sexes. Nowadays our view of such spectacles is a little distorted by the ferocious criticism of them by the Christian culture, which eventually led to their abolition. And the cruelty that characterized them during certain periods certainly made and makes it difficult to remember their originally sporting character. It is now generally acknowledged however that these "games" derived initially from an ancient form of funeral celebration like those recounted in the classical epics. And this aspect was never completely lost. The letter quoted earlier, which Pliny the Younger wrote to a prominent Veronese contemporary, mentions a spectacle organized at the Arena to honour the memory of his beloved wife. After congratulating the nobleman on the success of the event and the number of spectators it attracted Pliny tries to console him for the fact that the African panthers he had bought had failed to arrive in time for the *venatio* or big-game hunt he had planned as part of the proceedings.

The brave hunters and courageous combatants who took part in these entertainments were actually professional athletes engaged by wealthy impresarios, in much the same way as professional boxing and bull-fighting is run today. We must remember, however, that the Roman world was also a world of slavery, and the comparison soon breaks down. Nevertheless, like athletes of all periods, gladiators too had their following of fans and enjoyed enormous popularity, as can be deduced from various tombstone inscriptions and a series of mosiacs at the Verona Archaeological Museum which depict and even name combatants of the various categories (distinguished mainly on the basis of the weapons they wielded). The eloquently expressive Latin word for fans was *amatores*.

Having imagined the Arena in the splendour of its heyday, we are bound to be shocked by its subsequent decay, though

in actual fact, by comparison with other surviving Roman amphitheatres it has suffered much less, at least as regards the interior: it does still fulfil its theatrical function after all. But this relatively successful survival raises the question of why the monument should have undergone the severely mutilating loss of almost all its outer wall. The explanation usually given – that during the Middle Ages Roman monuments were treated as a ready source of half dressed stone – seems rather less than convincing, at least for Verona. From an archaeological point of view, Verona is one of the richest and most interesting of Roman cities, with a practically intact level of Roman remains beneath roads and built-up areas that faithfully reflect the lay-out of over two thousand years ago.

The Arco dei Gavi, a much easier prey for stone-hunters than the Arena, was demolished only in the late-1700s and was rebuilt with at least three quarters of the original materials in our own century. The city gates built at almost the same time as the Arena have survived in what archaeologists would call excellent condition, though the walls were extended several times during the Middle Ages. There are even substantial sections of the walls still standing. And the Roman theatre, which is older than the Arena and occupies a much more critical site, remains reasonably legible in all its parts.

On the other hand it is true that many of the city's mediaeval towers and house-towers are built on bases of stone taken from the Arena. So we can say that the Arena probably did become a source of building materials but only after a series of partial collapses due not to deliberate demolition but to various earthquakes, which struck Verona with particular intensity and frequency during the XII Cent.. The last, in 1223, was recorded on Christmas Day as a "tournament" was taking place in the Arena.

Support for this theory comes from the earliest "map" of Verona, the famous *Iconografia Rateriana*, named after Bishop Raterius, who lived in the X Cent.: the Arena is depicted intact, complete with the outer *ala* wall and the loggia in the interior, and enclosed within the city walls. We must remember too that during the darkest centuries of the early Middle Ages Verona was chosen as their capital by the Germanic tribes that then dominated Italy, and as the seat of their sovereigns, from Theodoric the Ostrogoth to Alboin, king of the Lombards and the Frankish king Pepin. Later the German emperors always paid great attention to the city that represented the first stage of their descents into Italy. So

Modern reproduction of the celebrated Iconography *of the city of Verona commissioned by Bishop Raterius in the X Cent. A.D..*

Opposite, detail of another reproduction of the Iconography.

Verona never sank into a period of complete decay but remained a city of solid stone buildings, made particularly of the pink stone known as Verona red. And the largest of these buildings, the Arena, was always treated with great care and respect. An early tradition actually names Theodoric as the founder of the "Labyrinth", as the Arena was sometimes called. And the *Iconografia Rateriana* contains the eloquent reference
Nobile, praecipuum, memorabile grande Theatrum,
Ad decus extructum sacra Verona tuum.
Nevertheless, it cannot be denied that the Arena gradually lost its function as an amphitheatre, the most disparate activities took root beneath its vaulting and it became home to many paupers and homeless. But even this process of occupation must have taken place to some extent under the control of the city authorities, who seem to have been imbued with a real sense of the Arena as an important item of public property requiring proper care and maintenance. This attitude emerges clearly from the municipal Statutes of the XIII Cent., which provide for an annual budget allocation for the purposes of restoring the Arena. And even when it is pointed out that there is historical evidence to show that the Arena was also used as a brothel in the Middle Ages, we must remember that it was the city authorities of the day who themselves institutionalized matters in this way in an attempt to ensure that prostitutes were confined to the *covoli* of the Arena, for which they also had to pay an appropriate rent.
Then during the Renaissance, interest in Verona's ancient monuments became very marked. The Arena, particularly was referred to, directly and indirectly, in many studies and paintings. From the mid-1400s we find a series of ordinances designed to prevent the uses and abuses to which the Arena was then subjected and to stop the monument being used as a source of building stone and as a rubbish dump. Following several attempts to repair the vaulting and especially to prevent the dangerous leakage of rainwater, the Council voted in 1568 to have the whole building restored; the protagonists of the operation are recorded on contemporary plaques as being the magistrates of the Republic of Venice, but in actual fact it was financed entirely by the artistocracy of Verona.
This was the most substantial, largest-scale work to be done on the Arena before our own age; it included the partial rebuilding of the tiered seating around the arena and the rebuilding of three upper arches which had collapsed into

Piazza Bra. This latter work was not undertaken however until after the interruption of 1575, when a serious plague outbreak resulted in the deaths of a fifth of the population. When Michel de Montaigne arrived in Verona in 1580 during his Italian journey, the great author of the *Essais* wrote of the Arena that it was the finest construction he had ever seen in his life. An appropriate note on which to close our brief survey of its history.

Overleaf, the Arena and the centre of Verona in a XIX Cent. engraving.

SPECTACLE AT THE ARENA

There exists no evidence, and not even a solid tradition, that any Christian met a martyr's death in the Arena. Stories abound of its having been the scene of trials by ordeal and trials by combat but these form part, together with knightly tournaments, of the mediaeval traditions of chivalry: romantic souls have stretched their vivid imaginations to picture the legendary Orlando, Rinaldo and even Sir Lancelot jousting there. Then there are much more probable stories of the Arena being used for judicial executions and it is unfortunately quite certain that 166 heretics were put to death there on 13th February 1278, during the crusade against the Albigensians.

It is highly likely that the Arena continued to be the regular setting for spectacular events of many kinds, entertaining and otherwise, during the centuries for which there is no direct record. We do know that part of the lavish celebrations for the wedding of Antonio della Scala to Samaritana da Polenta took place there and for 1382 there is an account of an entertainment which is highly evocative of the cultural climate of the late Middle Ages. A "Castle of Love" was erected in the Arena to hold the most beautiful maidens of the city, while bands of gentlemen from various cities, arrayed in ornate knightly costume, competed against each other to take it by storm. According to the account, the "entertainment" would have finished in a real battle, between the suitors of course, if the Lord of Verona had not pacified them with an invitation to them all to partake of a sumptuous banquet. This, like many other stories of joustings and tournaments, is so rich in detail that it gives the impression of having been invented, or at least embroidered somewhat.

For reliable reports of jousting tournaments we have to wait until the XVII Cent., but they were evidently rather empty, meretricious affairs and they soon fell from favour with the all-influential Arena audiences.

A more lasting tradition was established by the "Commedia", as the season of plays held in the Arena every summer was known for centuries. Every year, from the early 1700s, a small stage was rigged up on a wooden platform "and all the best companies in Italy took it is turns to show off their talents". The quotation comes from Carlo Goldoni's "Memoires", where he tells of the time he was the butt of laughter and derisory whistles from the Arena audience when the curtains parted too early after an interval and he was revealed still chatting to one of the actors. But that was before he became Italy's most famous playwright.

The "Commedia" was highly popular with the Veronese, also because ticket prices were really very low. Down in the arena, in the stalls as it were, one had to pay for a seat as well as for entrance, but up on the terraces one simply had to pay to get in, and then, as now, it was first come first served for the best places, though there was so much room it scarcely mattered. The impresarios to whom the municipal authorities leased the Arena for a fixed annual rent were contractually forbidden to raise the cost of the admission ticket. The repertory, provided by "companies of actors, acrobats and dancers" was quite catholic and catered to popular taste. Audiences too were wide-ranging, with entire tiers of monks and friars a common sight.

As well as the theatrical performances of the "Commedia" – mainly *commedia dell'arte*, ballet and circus acts – the Arena was occasionally used for bullfights, or rather bull-baiting. The dogs set on the bulls (or sometimes oxen) were trained by the butchers of the city, who normally used them to herd livestock to the slaughterhouse. But here the dogs themselves became the butchers, to the diversion of the crowd. Barbaric though it was, an "entertainment" of the kind was also put on in honour of Napoleon's visit to the Arena in 1805, but perhaps the day's prime crowd-puller on this occasion was really the Emperor of France.

Under the French, in the early 1800s, the "Commedia" continued to enjoy considerable success at the Arena. An inn-keeper of the day wrote of having been to the Arena to see "a most amusing play called 'Bonaparte in Egypt against the Mamelukes'. ... Wonderfully spectacular and extremely funny".

But Verona was shortly to become the city of the Restoration, with the last Congress of the Quadruple Alliance being held there in October-November 1822. To mark the occasion and to impress the gathered statesmen and crowned heads of Europe, a great campaign of restoration work on the fabric of the city itself was put in hand, the centrepiece being the transformation of Piazza Bra. The square was properly levelled out, all indecorous constructions were removed and the monumental Palazzo della Gran Guardia was completed. This was the time, too, when the authorities finally managed to clear the vaulted spaces beneath the arches around the ground floor of the Arena of all the workshops, shops and living quarters for which permits had been granted over the centuries. A ditch was dug around the Arena and dozens of huts and shacks clinging to the base of the *ala* were swept away.

Centre, the tiered seating of the Arena, looking towards the "ala".

Sides, the audience during an opera performance. As in other Roman amphitheatres, the Arena's striking beauty arises from the elegant simplicity of its elliptical curve, a shape that also has the functional advantage of offering excellent sight lines from all seats.

During the Congress "the days and weeks were spent in festivities, celebrations, banqueting, theatre-going, promenading and revelries, and Verona was in a state of perpetual exhilaration". Despite the lateness of the season, crowds flocked to the Arena on 25th November to see an extraordinary entertainment comprising a spectacularly choreographed "happening" designed to symbolize the benefits of the Restoration, preceded by a cantata bearing the equally allusive title of "The Sacred Alliance". The work was the brainchild of Metternich, who engaged Gioacchino Rossini to write and conduct the music, and the event in effect founded the tradition of opera perfomances at the Arena. Twenty years later, in July 1842, the same composer's celebrated *Stabat Mater* was given at the Arena after the performance at the Teatro Filarmonico ten days earlier had been sold out.

The nineteenth conception of restoration demanded that monuments be "freed" of all accretions and returned to what scholarly opinion held to be their original state. In pursuit of such aims, many monuments were, as it were, embalmed and isolated from their urban and social context. Sometimes the attitude even led to missing parts being added. The Arena was in danger of being treated in this light in the second half of the last century, when amongst the intentions of the project devised by Count Antonio Pompei was to completely rebuild the tiered seating around the arena, which had been remodelled during the period of Venetian domination of Verona. The proposals were fiercely debated in the city, but a quick and effective end was put to the controversy in 1882 when the Adige overflowed in a disastrous flood that shifted the city elders' efforts towards more immediate forms of reconstruction.

As for the pattern of entertainments following the Restoration, attempts were made under the Austrians to replace the cruel "sport" of bullbaiting with horseracing, and to give the events held there a socially useful character. Thus when the Austrian Emperor visited Verona, grand tombola sessions were organized at the Arena, with proceeds going to the creation of dowries for a certain number of poor young women. One imagines that the entertainment value of such sessions must have been rather low, but people nevertheless flocked there in their thousands in the hope of winning the lottery.

Despite the criticisms of the purists, who utterly rejected the idea of plays being presented at the Arena, theatrical activity continued to flourish there throughout the century. Indirect

attempts were made to suppress it by establishing other theatres in the city, including the still-extant Ristori in 1844 and the Nuovo in 1846. But the *teatrino* inside the Arena did not close down; indeed the stage was rebuilt after the fire that broke out during a performance of *The Capture of Sebastopol* in 1855. According to some sources, the fourteen-year-old Eleonora Duse made her début as Juliet there in 1897.

But of course the Arena was the scene of many other events as well as plays, from the magnificent occasion when Vittorio Emanuele II was present to acknowledge Verona's decision to join the Kingdom of Italy in 1866 to other spectacular affairs such as the launching of hot-air balloons and early bicycle races. The first experiments in turning the Arena into a regular venue for opera took place in 1856 with performances of *Il casino di campagna* and *La fanciulla di Gand* by the local composer Pietro Lenotti, followed by *Le convenienze teatrali* and *I pazzi per progetto* by Donizetti. But the real dawn of the tradition of opera at the Arena came in 1913 with the celebrated production of *Aida*. With its opera season, the Arena has rediscovered a function worthy of its quality as a historic monument and at the same time consonant with its origins as a place of spectacular public entertainment. It is important to remember however that the events held there must never be allowed to dictate the uses to which the Arena is put. The priority at all times must be the historical integrity and physical safety of Verona's most famous monument.

THE ARENA
AND OPERA

Remo Schiavo

*The cast lists for operas and ballets
all refer to the first night performance.*

OPERA SEASONS AND PERSONALITIES FROM 1913 TO THE 1980s

The Verona Arena cannot boast the long history of association with opera that is the pride of so many Italian theatres. But though it became a regular venue only in 1913 and suffered inevitable interruptions during wartime, its history offers a fascinating cross-section of Italian opera which, after its heyday in the 1700s and most of the 1800s was already showing signs of crisis by the beginning of our own century. Since then the creative vigour of opera in Italy has dwindled still further and the art form lives on only through the glories of the past, happily supported by an ever-growing public which retains its ability to discriminate between the virtues of a product assembled in the recording studio and the altogether more exciting experience of a live performance, with all its potential for indescribable elation and bitter disappointment. The choice of *Aida* for the celebrations at the Arena to commemorate the hundredth anniversary of the birth of Giuseppe Verdi was certainly not a matter of chance. Of all the operas composed by the Maestro, only *Aida* would be able to escape being overwhelmed by the sheer size of the Arena. As Teodor Mommsen put it to Quintino Sella, "one doesn't go to Rome to accomplish matters of petty routine," so there is no point in using the Arena only to express the intimate ferment of the human soul; such ferment must of course be present, as it is present in every poetic work, but for the Arena there must be an explosion of solar light, the action must identify with the sea of stone surrounding it, there must be a perfect fusion of the fictitious world of the story being played out on the stage and the real, here and now world of the audience. It was the choice of that first *Aida* and its astonishing success that underlay the policy decisions of the future years. It gave rise to the idea of a certain sort of opera as being suitable for the Arena, and by extension of certain sorts of voices, and the constant claim was that Arena audiences would see and experience something that no other Italian opera house could offer. Yet the architects of the triumph, conductor Tullio Serafin, soprano Ester Mazzoleni and mezzo Maria Gay Zenatello, never forgot that *Aida* is Verdi's only opera to start and finish with a *pianissimo*, and that the crowd scenes are precisely balanced with scenes of passionate lyricism. A certain kind of audience responded to the exhilarating drama of the *concertati* numbers in the triumphal scene while more refined souls rhapsodized over the soft pizzicato of the violins in the description of the banks of the Nile or over the exquisite blend of soprano and clarinet in "Cieli azzurri".

The 1913 production of Verdi's Aida: *the poster and a photograph of the first night. The poster design depicts the presentation of the sword to Radames against a background of the Arena looking towards the "ala".*

And here it became apparent that a second miracle had been wrought: by some mysterious combination of acoustic factors the ancient stones of the amphitheatre reflected sound with the same limpid perfection as that achieved by Bibiena, Piermarini, Mauro and the other great Italian theatre designers of the XVIII Cent. The opera-spectacle chosen for the following season (1914) was *Carmen*, in a perhaps almost deliberate attempt to stave off the looming horrors of the Great War with an invitation to plunge instead into the world of gypsies, smugglers, bull-fighters and the girls from the tobacco factory. Ettore Fagiuoli, who had designed the bold sets used for *Aida*, seems to have turned in on himself, creating an enclosed scene between Moorish-style pillars and hiding the tiered sweep of the amphitheatre behind the stage with trees or flats depicting the city gate. In 1919, the Arena reopened after the War with Amilcare Ponchielli's *Figliol prodigo*. This was the first and only production of the unwieldy work at the Arena, and its disappearance from the repertoire aroused no searing regret, despite Ettore Panizza's excellent conducting, a committed team of singers (though none of them had real star quality), Fagiuoli's impressive scenery and the thrilling dancing of Teresa Battagi, the prima ballerina. In 1920 the decision to put on two operas - *Aida* and *Mefistofele* - marked the beginning of a proper annual series of operas and renewed acknowledgement of a point made first in 1913 - that opera at the Arena needs big-name singers. Nazzareno De Angelis, Aureliano Pertile and Bianca Scacciati starred in Boito's *Mefistofele* while Tina Poli Randaccio, Giuseppina Zinetti and Alessandro Dolci took the leads in *Aida*. Fine singers they all were, certainly, but with voices suited to the Arena? The robust bass De Angelis certainly conformed to the stereotype, as did the impetuous Poli Randaccio, but Scacciati and Pertile were stylists, belcanto artists of a high order. Nevertheless their voices carried to the furthest reaches of the amphitheatre. Slowly it began to sink in that voices of exceptional power and athleticism were not needed in the Arena: it was enough to sing well and clearly. Focal point of the 1921 season was the composer Pietro Mascagni, who conducted a remarkable twelve performances of his *Piccolo Marat*. This was not however a sign that the Arena was willing to risk productions of new works as yet unendorsed by popular success: Mascagni, who had composed *Cavalleria rusticana* back in 1890, was currently the best-loved musician in Italy and the leading role was sung by the magnificent Spanish tenor Hipolito

Opposite: top, a preparatory drawing by Ettore Fagiuoli for Act III, Scene II of the 1921 Samson et Dalila *by Saint-Saëns; below, another drawing by Fagiuoli, for Act II of the 1922 production of Wagner's* Lohengrin. *More an architect than a painter, Fagiuoli tends always to relate his scenery designs to their monumental backdrop.*

Overleaf, one of Fagiuoli's drawings for Massenet's Le Roi de Lahore *for the 1923 season. As usual, Fagiuoli relies on architectural constructions rather than painted flats for his Hindu temple.*

ATTO III° SANSONE E DALILA · SCENA FINALE

Lazaro. But with *Marat* it was clear that the history of Italian opera had come to an end (with just one exception - Puccini's *Turandot* - but that still had to be written). In 1922, Wagner made his entrance into the Arena with *Lohengrin*. Tullio Serafin was again in charge, and it was assumed that since the supporters of Wagner and those of Verdi had tired of their fierce rivalries, works by the two composers could comfortably be given on equal terms in the same Arena season. But even if we admit that a *Lohengrin* conducted by Serafin could establish itself in the affections of Italian opera-goers, especially when sung by Aureliano Pertile and Ezio Pinza (and singers of such quality are simply not around today), it is abundantly clear that three quarters of a century later Wagner is only an occasional presence in Italy and at the Arena the duel between the German and Italian champions finished long ago with a crushing victory for Verdi. In the following year, 1923, the Arena again offered an opera that was rarely produced elsewhere, *Le Roi de Lahore* by Massenet, an elegant French confection presented by Ettore Panizza. Again an interesting but unsuccessful attempt to expand the repertoire, for after the Arena production the story of the Hindu prince disappeared completely from the Italian stage. 1924 brought another bold stroke with a production of Richard Wagner's *Parsifal*. Now that Bayreuth had loosened its grip on Wagner's operas, all the Italian opera houses were falling over themselves to put on the master's last work: not to have a production of *Parsifal* amounted to *lèse culture*. But the Arena *Parsifal* failed to draw the crowds, even though it had Sergio Failoni on the podium and Kundry was the legendary Maria Leacer, a soprano with a piercing top C as superhumanly true as the blade of Siegfried's sword. The 1924 programme also featured *Andrea Chénier* for the first time, with Francesco Merli as Andrea, and the opera scored an immediate triumph. The following year saw one of those occasions when an opera seems to owe its success above all to one singer: the opera was Rossini's *Mosè* and the singer the bass Nazzareno De Angelis, the very incarnation of Michelangelo's celebrated marble statue. Also in 1925, Giannina Arangi Lombardi and Irene Minghini Cattaneo unsheathed metaphorical lionesses' claws for their roles in Ponchielli's *La Gioconda*. The Arena continued to administer the kiss of death to its unusual revivals in the Summer of 1926 with a production of Arrigo Boito's *Nerone*; it had been saved at La Scala by Toscanini and Pertile, but despite the conducting skills of Gaetano

Above, Ettore Fagiuoli, scenery design for Act III of Andrea Chénier *by* Giordano (1924).

Opposite, Ettore Fagiuoli, design for Act II of Verdi's Aida (1927).

Bavagnoli the Arena audience were bored to the point of polite intolerance. Far better to submit to the sure appeal of *Il trovatore* and be thrilled by John Sullivan's ringing high Cs. The Venetian conductor Antonio Guarnieri had let it be known in previous years that the proper activity for open-air entertainment was playing bowls, but in 1927 he was so impressed by the acoustics of the Arena that he agreed to take up the baton not only for *Aida* but also for Gaspare Spontini's *La vestale* and a Beethoven concert containing both the 5th and 9th Symphonies. And if he had any lingering doubts about how a *pianissimo* can carry across the Arena Giannina Arangi Lombardi's beautifully floated notes in "Cieli azzurri" will finally have convinced him. The end of the 1920s was enlivened by the duel between the two greatest tenors of the day, Giacomo Lauri Volpi and Beniamino Gigli. Nowadays such a contest would seem ridiculous because the two voices were so utterly different:

L'OPERA "TVRANDOT.. NE L'ARENA DI VERON

Lauri Volpi was the heir of Arturo Rubini; Gigli of the more recent Enrico Caruso. In 1928, *Turandot*, Giacomo Puccini's final effort and in effect the swan-song too of Italian opera, made its first appearance at the Arena. Lauri Volpi, dropped by Toscanini at La Scala in favour of the Spaniard Miguel Fleta, immediately engaged to sing Calaf in Verona and the heroic fervour of his "Vincerò" will have overcome any resistance the Icy Princess might have offered. That memorable season also offered Lauri Volpi's celebrated portrait of the Duke of Mantua, a figure at once exciting and disturbing, an authentic lesson in Renaissance sybaritism. It was Beniamino Gigli's turn to impress the following season (1929) with an opera that has now all but disappeared from the repertoire: *Marta* by Friedrich von Flotow. Gigli had just the right physique and voice for Lionello, who falls in love with the princess disguised as a peasant girl, to whom he sings the famous "M'appari tutta amor". The two

Centre, drawing for Act II of the 1928 production of Puccini's Turandot. *Though he remained faithful to a clear set of aesthetic principles in his scenery designs for the Arena, Fagiuoli managed successfully to embrace the exoticism of* Aida, *the Celestial Empire of Turandot's China and the Tribunal of revolutionary Paris.*

performances Gigli gave were both sold out ages before the day and followed by scenes of wild enthusiasm at the stage door, but it bears remembering that the season also featured Hipolito Lazaro as Folco in Mascagni's *Isabeau*, Ezio Pinza and Gina Cigna in Gounod's *Faust* and Gianna Pederzini as Nancy in *Marta*. Arena audiences saw *Boris Godunov* for the first time in 1930, with bass Ezio Pinza outstanding in the tragic role of the unhappy Czar. On the first night a shooting star streaked across the sky just as the Czar was dying, prompting conductor Gianandrea Gavazzeni to comment: "An excellent sense of the theatrical, that fellow God!". Together with the Mussorgsky, the 1930 programme contained a memorable *Forza del destino* with Bianca Scacciati, Carlo Tagliabue, Francesco Merli, Ezio Pinza and Ebe Stignani, and Giuseppe Del Campo conducting. The 1931 programme was an adventurous one with Wagner's *Die Meistersinger von Nürnberg*, Rossini's *Guglielmo Tell* and Boito's *Mefistofele*. The Wagner was still sung in Italian, the *Tell* earned its place in the Arena on the grounds of the opportunities it offers for impressive scenery (again by Ettore Fagiuoli) and *Mefistofele* was still in favour in Italy. Gigli paid another visit in 1932 to sing in Meyerbeer's *L'Africaine* and his exquisitely gentle rendering of "Le Paradis" (in Italian of course) brought the house down. Aureliano Pertile gave his stylish Riccardo in *Un ballo in maschera* in the same season: no show-stopping moments but indisputably a superlative exhibition of *belcanto* singing. And in danger of passing unnoticed amid the great names, the unmistakable art and beauty of Margherita Carosio in the part of the page Oscar. The duel between Gigli and Lauri Volpi continued over the next few years. Meyerbeer's *Les Huguenots* was given its one and only production at the Arena in 1933, and alongside an incomparable throng of enthralling voices Lauri Volpi ravished the ear with enchanting performances of the romance "Plus blanche que la blanche hermine" and in "Tu l'as dit: oui tu m'aimes". Aureliano Pertile repeated his 1922 Lohengrin and Francesco Merli sang a heroic Manrico in *Il Trovatore*, but in the history of the Arena, 1933 is and will remain the year of *Les Huguenots*. 1934, on the other hand, was the year of Beniamino Gigli, who sang in the opera in which he made his debut in Rovigo, *La Gioconda*, and in *Andrea Chénier* with Maria Caniglia. But also to be heard in that year was another living legend, Toti Dal Monte, whose *Lucia di Lammermoor* had her audiences in raptures and proved beyond doubt that the Arena will thrill

Ettore Fagiuoli's design for Act I of the 1931 production of Wagner's Die Meistersinger von Nürnberg. *The sketch provides further proof of the inexhaustible eclecticism of his astonishing evocation of mediaeval Germany.*

ARENA DI VERONA·ESTATE 1931·I MAESTRI CANTORI·ATTO 1°
- ARCH. ETTORE FAGIVOLI -

1 Giugno 1921

just as readily to the diaphanous threads of sound, the trills and soaring arabesques of the Mad Scene and its glittering rondo as for high Cs from Lauri Volpi or Maria Leacer. The 1935 season offered a courageous programme, with the guaranteed drawing power of *Norma* and *Cavalleria rusticana* balanced by three rarities: Catalani's *Loreley*, Rimsky-Korsakov's *Shéhérazade* and *La Resurrezione di Cristo* by Lorenzo Perosi. And the cast lists contained not only established stars such as Merli, Pasero and Stignani but also the up-and-coming, including Gina Cigna, Lina Bruna Rasa, Licia Albanese and Galliano Masini, the acknowledged heir apparent of both Gigli and Lauri Volpi. He returned in 1936 to sing Radames, while Tito Schipa and Margherita Carosio were engaged for the delightful *L'elisir d'amore*. This was Schipa's first experience of the Arena and there was considerable interest in how his light lyric tenor voice would cope with the vastness of the open-air amphitheatre. But when he sang "Furtiva lacrima" at the beginning of the opera, it was already clear that the curve of the Arena provided the perfect sounding board for his voice. From 1937 until the opera season was suspended for the duration of the War, the dominating figure at the Arena was the phenomenal Giuseppe Lugo. He was from Verona and combined an appealing personality and pleasing appearance with a pure lyric tenor voice and effortlessly sound technique. In the 1937 *Tosca* he established an unassailable reputation as the leading Cavaradossi of the day, and there are still those who talk in awed tones of how his ringing "Vittoria" resounded on the far side of Piazza Bra. His Tosca was the already famous Gina Cigna, whose forthcoming Turandot was to remain unrivalled until the advent of Maria Callas. But a glance at the cast lists for 1937 will show how many other young stars were also beginning to shine. *Mefistofele*, in which Tancredi Pasero sang the lead to open the season, also featured Pia Tassinari and Gabriella Gatti, and Mafalda Favero made her debut as Liù in *Turandot*, all three of them extremely beautiful women as well as incomparable singers. Obviously Lugo was asked back for the 1937 season, this time to sing to packed houses in *La Bohème* beside Mafalda Favero, the most exquisitely perfect Mimì of her time. Carlo Tagliabue and Tancredi Pasero also enjoyed triumphal receptions in *Nabucco*, as did Ebe Stignani and Giovanni Malipiero in *La Favorita* and Sergio Failoni conducting Wagner's *Tannhäuser* in the only Arena production it has so far been given. The War was close now, but before the enforced

Ettore Fagiuoli's design for Act I of La Gioconda *by Amilcare Ponchielli (1934). Fagiuoli boldly shifts the setting from the courtyard of the Doge's Palace to the Piazetta outside, viewed from between the columns of St. Mark and St. Theodore to give dramatic emphasis to the bulk of the Doge's Palace, the side of St. Mark's Basilica and a section of the lagoonside wharf in the foreground.*

IA — GIOCONDA — ATTO 1°   11 giugno 1922

closure came the Arena put on one last, unforgettable season, with Lugo in *Rigoletto* and *Tosca*, beside the enchanting Gilda of Margherita Carosio and the fiery and passionate Floria Tosca of Maria Caniglia. Mafalda Favero was an affecting Marguerite in Gounod's *Faust* and Gabriella Gatti a convincing Juliet in Zandonai's *Giulietta e Romeo*. The wartime blackout lasted until 1946, and there were anxious moments for the Arena too as the Allies rained bombs and incendiary devices down on the city. Indeed a bomb is reported to have fallen on the ancient Roman monument, but it luckily had about as much effect as a midge on an elephant. With the War over and *joie de vivre* possible once more, the Arena, *semper eadem*, already managed to offer *Aida* and *La traviata* in Summer 1946. The part of Radames was shared by Galliano Masini and the young Mario Del Monaco. 1947 saw other celebrated debuts: Maria Callas in *La Gioconda*, Renata Tebaldi in Gounod's *Faust* and Nicola Rossi Lemeni in both. Again, only a few experts realized that these were the voices on which the fate of Italian opera would rest for the next decade and more; most pined for the glories of the 1930s, Lauri Volpi, Gigli, Caniglia and Pasero, who were still in fine form but were unaffordable on the tight post-war budget. The rapid rise of the formidable Callas continued in 1948 with a *Turandot* of unequalled vocal power and dramatic strength, and Nicola Rossi Lemeni - Timur in *Turandot* and Don Basilio in *Il barbiere di Siviglia* - also sustained his advance. *Otello* and *Carmen* saw the debut of the Chilean tenor Ramon Vinay, a tenor with a baritonal colour to his voice that gave him the ideal dramatic weight for the role of tragic hero. Giuletta Simonato also stepped onto the Arena stage for the first time in 1948, and gave a sparkling, silvery Rosina in *Il barbiere*. Attempts were made in 1949 to placate those still yearning to hear the great pre-War voices, but Lauri Volpi had some difficulty with *Rigoletto* and withdrew from *Il trovatore*, though Carlo Tagliabue as Rigoletto and Ebe Stignani as Azucena enjoyed enthusiastic acclaim. It was the younger generation of singers who aroused most enthusiasm on the terraces, however: for Tebaldi as a sweetly gentle Elsa in *Lohengrin*, singing opposite Boris Christoff as Heinrich. In 1950 Beniamino Gigli made a triumphal return in *La forza del destino* (the press joked that Verona would have to enlarge the Arena if he came again), but the celebrated tenor was now over sixty and he abandoned *La Bohème* to Giuseppe Di Stefano, one of the new talents (along with Gino Penno

Two drawings, by Ettore Fagiuoli and Vittorio Filippini, for the 1948 opera season: above, for Act II of Bizet's Carmen, *and below, for Act I of* Il barbiere di Siviglia *by Rossini.*

in *Die Walküre*) who made their mark that year. During the rest of the 1950s programmes were dominated by Mario Del Monaco, Maria Callas in *La traviata* and *La Gioconda*, Nicola Rossi Lemeni with his deeply tragic Boris and Magda Olivero's sweetly poignant Liù and her sensual Manon. The repertoire covered at the Arena continued to shrink during the decade: Verdi held his own but Wagner disappeared entirely. Audience discussion no longer centred on the opera but on the scenery and singers, chief of whom towards the end of the '50s were Ettore Bastianini, Carlo Bergonzi, Franco Corelli, Anita Cerquetti, Antonietta Stella and Giulietta Simionato. Black American soprano Leontyne Price made just two appearances at the Arena, in *Aida* and *Il trovatore*, but they left an indelible mark. Magda Olivero gave every sign of being immune to the passing of the years and her vocal technique continued to astound, while important new names included Renata Scotto, Leyla Gencer and Virginia Zeani. A new feature of 1960s programmes

One of Pier Luigi Pizzi's sets for the 1969 production of Puccini's Turandot. *The striking basic design was adapted for use in all three acts, colour being used to excellent effect, especially the aquamarine of Acts I and III.*

was the inclusion of ballet. In the early years dance programmes were entrusted to the *corps de ballet* of La Scala, but the Marynski Ballet Company from St. Petersburg in 1966 and the Kiev Ballet in 1967 gave inimitable expression of the still vital traditions of the Russian school. Now came the era of Carla Fracci, first with the American Theater Ballet, then with the *corps de ballet* of La Scala, and finally with the Arena company. 1969 was an exceptional year by any standards, offering a *Turandot* with Birgit Nilsson and Placido Domingo, and a *Don Carlo* with Domingo, Caballé, Cappuccilli and Cossotto in a memorable production by Jean Vilar. In the 1970s there were innumerable revivals of Aida but also excellent productions of lesser-known Verdi operas such as *Nabucco*, *I Lombardi*, *Attila*, *Simon Boccanegra* and *Macbeth*. Those who believed that *Turandot* was the only Puccini opera that should be attempted at the Arena had to admit the regular appearance and equally regular success of *Manon Lescaut*, *Madama Butterfly*, *La Bohème* and obviously *Tosca*. Among the distinguished singers who first appeared at the Arena during the 1970s were Luciano Pavarotti, who made his Arena debut in 1972 in *Un ballo in maschera*, Gianfranco Cecchele, a perfect don Alvaro in *La forza del destino*, Renato Bruson, ideal in *Macbeth*, Bonaldo Gaiotti, Giacomo Aragall, Raina Kabaivanska and Ghena Dimitrova. Verona continues to see many other important debuts. It will be for a future history of opera at the Arena to record their names.

A drawing by Pino Casarini for Act II of the 1966 production of Verdi's Aida. *Casarini tends always to go for colourful, large-scale pictorial effect, full of well-judged detail.*

THE OPERAS OF GIUSEPPE VERDI

To say Verdi and to say the Arena di Verona is one and the same thing. Indeed there would be no tradition of opera at the Arena if the tenor Giovanni Zenatello had not had the idea of commemorating the hundredth anniversary of the composer's birth with a production of *Aida* there in 1913; and similarly *Aida* would no longer be *Aida* if it lacked its associations with the Arena. Foreigners might justifiably question Italians' devotion to Verdi were it not that the high point of almost every season in their own opera houses is also a work by Verdi. But for Italians, Verdi means something more than the composer of some of our culture's best known and best loved music. Verdi was born in 1813 and died in 1901, so his long life spanned the entire period of the Risorgimento, the movement which led to the political unification of Italy in the second half of the century. Verdi was by nature too sceptical to stoop to composing works of political propaganda, but it is undeniable that from *Nabucco* on, at least until *Aida*, the ideas that inspired the composer coincided with the thinking of the philosophers, politicians and poets who made Italy. Almost all the operas contain an aria, a line, a chorus in which Verdi's contemporaries detected a clearly political reference. *Aida*, which was being written as the age-old power of the Popes was coming to an end and France was succumbing to the military might of the Prussian armies, seems to be a response not to the triumphant completion of Italian unification but to the end of a heroic era and the advance of a negative, nihilistic philosophy which foresaw the end of the "old" Europe. Verdi's pessimism develops further in *Otello* and *Falstaff*. Though *Otello* does explore the idea that evil might be just the capricious result of sheer, purposeless desire to do evil, the great fugue finale of *Falstaff* makes merciless fun of every human aspiration, amorous, economic and even ethical. There is however a view that all Verdi's works are imbued with an at least formal Catholicism, a theory that leads of course to the *Requiem*, where the pessimism of the "Dies Irae" is offset by the overriding comprehensiveness of God's forgiveness. The first appearance of *Aida* at the Arena dates from 1913, when Italian critical opinion was prepared to countenance none of Verdi's works except for *Otello* and *Falstaff*, and those only because they were redolent of Wagner. The triumph scored by *Aida* with those early productions at the Arena underlined the fact that Verdi was still regarded with great affection by Italians (who have never paid the slightest attention to the critics); and the

success of *Aida* led to enthusiastic Arena revivals not only of works with potentially spectacular crowd scenes like *La forza del destino*, but also of more intimate operas such as *Rigoletto*, *La traviata*, *Il trovatore* and *Simon Boccanegra*. But *Aida* has always held the record for the overall number of performances and for sold out performances, hence the successful insistence by the tourist agencies and certain journalists that the opera should feature in every season's programme. The *Aida*s of the 1980s were almost all revivals of the legendary 1913 production. Gianfranco De Bosio launched the idea in 1982, and the resulting performances were at once spectacular, fascinating and invigorating; reconstructions of Fagiuoli's mobile, 3-dimensional scenery in particular showed that sooner or later the designer of any production intended for the Arena must come to terms with the monumental size and nature of the setting. Auguste Mariette's costumes too have stood the test of time. Among the most frequent members of alternating casts were Maria Chiara and Nicola Martinucci as Aida and Radames, and Fiorenza Cossotto, Bruna Baglioni and several other more or less famous mezzosopranos in the part of Amneris. In 1987 and 1988, wedged between the De Bosio revival years, was a futuristic new production by Pietro Zuffi with scenery and costumes that looked as if they had been designed by computer. More faithful to the spirit of Verdi's music and absolutely respectful of the Arena as a Roman monument was Vittorio Rossi's 1990 production. In the light of the setting sun bathing the pink stone of the amphitheatre Rossi's sets seemed to rise as if from a stepped pyramid. Several other Verdi operas have appeared beside *Aida* over the last decade. We turn first to *Otello* (1982) because productions of the opera at the Arena have been rare, particularly in view of the difficulty in engaging a Moor of Venice with the right kind of heroic tenor voice. Vittorio Rossi's scenery successfully bridged the visual gap between a Roman amphitheatre in Verona and the Venetian fortifications in Cyprus; Vladimir Atlantov's Otello was more convincing in the lyric parts of his role than the dramatic; and Kiri Te Kanawa was an elegant and sweet-toned Desdemona. The other Verdi opera in 1982 was *Macbeth*. Renzo Giacchieri's production scarcely bothered with scenery and relied for its effect on the brilliant costumes designed by Ferruccio Villagrossi and on the powerful Macbeth of Renato Bruson, with Ghena Dimitrova and Bonaldo Giaiotti. One of the Arena's really important achievements was its extremely successful production of *I*

Lombardi alla prima Crociata, an early opera which is usually remembered only for its famous chorus "O Signore, dal tetto natio". Attilio Colonnello's scenery alluded to the Romanesque-Gothic mosaics and stained glass of mediaeval Lombardy with striking effect; bass Ruggero Raimondi triumphed as Pagano and received exemplary support from the fine voices of Veriano Luchetti and Katia Ricciarelli. Any season aspiring to present *Il trovatore* must be able to count on an outstanding tenor, a real star who can electrify the audience when it comes to "Di quella pira". In 1985, Franco Bonisolli hurled a phenomenal four high Cs into the skies over the Arena, but this *Trovatore* will be remembered more for Mario Ceroli's Simone Martini – inspired sets and for the scrupulous production of Giuseppe Patroni Griffi. The praiseworthy policy of presenting Verdi's lesser-known operas at the Arena paid off handsomely in 1986 with a well-received *Attila* sung by Yevgeny Nestorenko, Maria Chiara and Veriano Luchetti, conducted by Nello Santi and produced by Giuliano Montaldo. Also in 1986, *Un ballo in maschera* was given the full Arena treatment with a thrilling explosion of light and colour for the ball in the last act. Production, scenery and costumes were all by Pietro Zuffi and Gustav Kuhn was an excellent conductor but this *Ballo* nevertheless failed to displace an earlier version starring Luciano Pavarotti in the hearts of Arena regulars. Even "ordinary" opera houses think twice before putting *La traviata* so one can imagine the apprehension at the Arena, where memories of the achingly credible Violettas of Maria Callas and Magda Olivero are still very much alive. The 1987 production aroused considerable controversy at its first night, but subsequent performances were politely applauded. Strangely, one of the Arena's soaring successes of the early '90s has been *Nabucco*, which the critics place firmly amongst Verdi's minor operas. Sold-out signs to rival *Aida*, revivals in successive seasons and soul-stirring performances of "Va' pensiero", with the chorus mingling with the audience for the inevitable encores (a crowd-pleasing idea of conductor Daniel Oren). *La forza del destino* made a welcome return in 1989, with the splendid Maria Chiara and Giuseppe Giacomini in the lead roles and young bass Roberto Scandiuzzi scoring a notable success. Conductor Alexander Lazarev drew brilliantly colourful performances of the score from the orchestra and Sandro Bolchi's production made the most of the crowd scenes. No overview of Verdi works presented at the Arena can ignore the frequent performances of the *Messa da requiem*, given in six seasons between 1966 and 1990. Prior to 1980 the *Requiem* was greeted rather passively by the audiences, but in that year Riccardo Muti unleashed a positive passion for "sacred" Verdi and the great phalanx of the orchestra, the chorus banked around the stage, soloists Caballé, Fassbaender, Luchetti and Raimondi and the famous conductor himself were given an ovation of a length and intensity that are rare even in the Arena. The *Requiem* was a huge success again in 1986 under Daniel Oren and in 1990 under Lorin Maazel, but audience attention was perhaps concentrated rather on Luciano Pavarotti, whose appearances at the Arena have prompted something of a return to the *divismo* of the 1930s.

A violoncello resting between acts: one of the traditional but always moving experiences for members of the audience with seats in the stalls is to move to the front of the arena during the interval and gaze down into the vast, empty orchestra pit.

AIDA
1 9 8 2
Reconstruction of the 1913 production

King of Egypt	Alfredo Zanazzo
Amneris	Fiorenza Cossotto
Aida	Maria Chiara
Radames	Nicola Martinucci
Ramfis	Ferruccio Furlanetto
Amonasro	Alessandro Cassis
Conductor	Nello Santi
Producer	Gianfranco De Bosio
Choreography	Susanna Egri
Designer	Vittorio Rossi
(after sets by Ettore Fagiuoli	
and costumes by Auguste Mariette)	
Chorus master	Corrado Mirandola

Scenery, costumes and production were all faithful reproductions of those of the Arena's memorable first Aida of 1913. In the last scene a halo of light isolates Aida and Radames from the temple and the vast stone amphitheatre to evoke the flight of their souls "to the glow of eternal day".

AIDA
1 9 8 3
Reconstruction of the 1913 production

King of Egypt	ALFREDO ZANAZZO
Amneris	FIORENZA COSSOTTO
Aida	MARIA CHIARA
Radames	ERNESTO VERONELLI
Ramfis	BONALDO GIAIOTTI
Amonasro	GIUSEPPE SCANDOLA
Conductor	NELLO SANTI
Producer	GIANFRANCO DE BOSIO
Choreography	SUSANNA EGRI
Designer	VITTORIO ROSSI
(after sets by Ettore Fagiuoli	
and costumes by Auguste Mariette)	
Chorus master	CORRADO MIRANDOLA

The columns provide imposing backgrounds for the great crowd scenes and private spaces for the more intimate scenes. Fagiuoli's three-dimensional scenery enabled the 1913 audience also to fill the tiered seating at the back of the stage. The palette of colours the designer used reflected his scrupulous research among the temples of Ancient Egypt.

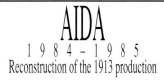

AIDA

1 9 8 4 - 1 9 8 5

Reconstruction of the 1913 production

1 9 8 4

King of Egypt	GIOVANNI GUSMEROLI
Amneris	FIORENZA COSSOTTO
Aida	MARIA CHIARA
Radames	NICOLA MARTINUCCI
Ramfis	BONALDO GIAIOTTI
Amonasro	GIANPIERO MASTROMEI
Conductor	PETER MAAG
Producer	GIANFRANCO DE BOSIO
Choreoraphy	SUSANNA EGRI
Designer	VITTORIO ROSSI
(after sets by Ettore Fagiuoli	
and costumes by Auguste Mariette)	
Chorus master	TULLIO BONI

1 9 8 5

King of Egypt	ALFREDO ZANAZZO
Amneris	BRUNA BAGLIONI
Aida	MAKVALA KASRASHVILI
Radames	GIUSEPPE GIACOMINI
Ramfis	BONALDO GIAIOTTI
Amonasro	GIUSEPPE SCANDOLA
Conductor	DANIEL OREN
Producer	GIANFRANCO DE BOSIO
Choreography	SUSANNA EGRI
Designer	VITTORIO ROSSI
Chorus master	TU⋯ BONI

AIDA
1986-1987

1986

King of Egypt	FRANCO FEDERICI
Amneris	FIORENZA COSSOTTO
Aida	NATALYA TROITSKAYA
Radames	FRANCO BONISOLLI
Ramfis	BONALDO GIAIOTTI
Amonasro	CORNELL MC NEIL
Conductor	DANIEL OREN
Producer	GIANFRANCO DE BOSIO
Designer	VITTORIO ROSSI

(after sets by Ettore Fagiuoli
and costumes by Auguste Mariette)

Choreography	SUSANNA EGRI
Chorus master	ALDO DANIELI

1987

King of Egypt	CARLO DEL BOSCO
Amneris	FIORENZA COSSOTTO
Aida	MARIA CHIARA
Radames	NICOLA MARTINUCCI
Ramfis	BONALDO GIAIOTTI
Amonasro	PIERO CAPPUCCILLI
Conductor	DONATO RENZETTI
Production	PIETRO ZUFFI
Designer	PIETRO ZUFFI
Choreography	MARIO PISTONI
Chorus master	ALDO DANIELI

Pietro Zuffi's scenery and costumes for the 1987 Aida *prompted lively debate among Arena habitués. Original rather than extravagant, wholly consistent and deriving from the rational, mathematical motif of the pyramid, the scenery followed the curve of the amphitheatre, crowned by the sun at the height of the Triumphal Scene.*

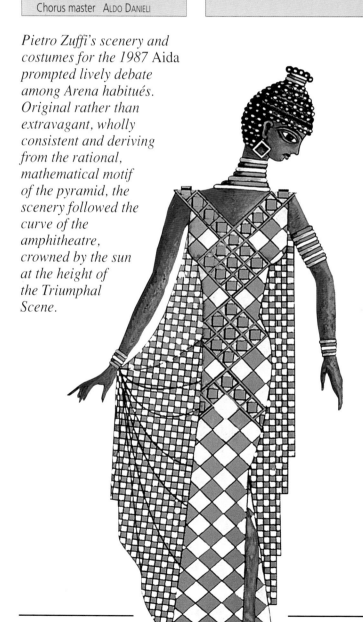

AIDA
1 9 8 6 - 1 9 8 7

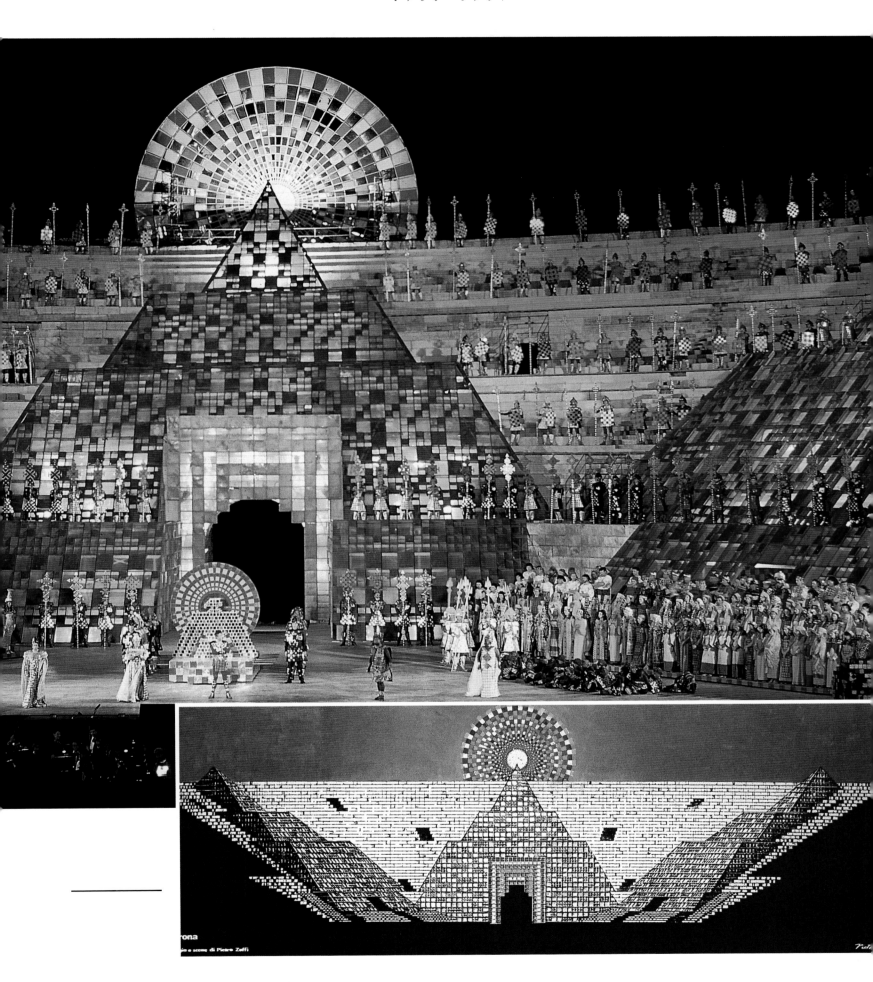

King of Egypt	CARLO DE BORTOLI
Amneris	FIORENZA COSSOTTO
Aida	MARIA CHIARA
Radames	FRANCO BONISOLLI
Ramfis	FRANCESCO ELLERO D'ARTEGNA
Amonasro	PIERO CAPPUCCILLI
Conductor	DONATO RENZETTI
Production	PIETRO ZUFFI
Designer	PIETRO ZUFFI
Choreography	MARIO PISTONI
Chorus master	ALDO DANIELI

At the end of the opera Pietro Zuffi's three pyramids slowly took on an incandescent glow as if they were being consumed by a blaze within, a highly effective visual metaphor for the sacrifice of the two lovers "beneath the altar of the outraged god".

RADAMES II° ATTO (TRIONFO)

RADAMES INCORONATO

AIDA
1 9 8 9
Reconstruction of the 1913 production

King of Egypt	Alfredo Zanazzo
Amneris	Bruna Baglioni
Aida	Aprile Millo
Radames	Bruno Beccaria
Ramfis	Francesco Ellero D'Artegna
Amonasro	Garbis Boyagian
Conductor	Pinchas Steinberg
Producer	Gianfranco De Bosio
Designer	Vittorio Rossi
Choreography	Susanna Egri
Chorus master	Aldo Danieli

Between the too many Aidas of Ettore Fagiuoli and the two of Pietro Zuffi came Vittorio Rossi's, perhaps the most perfect of all and the closest to the architectural simplicity of the Roman amphitheatre.
The predominant colour in this production was pink, reflecting the colour of the marble used for the Arena and quarried in nearby Valpolicella.

Below, Ivo Vinco as Ramfis.

AIDA
1 9 9 0

King of Egypt	ALFREDO ZANAZZO
Amneris	FIORENZA COSSOTTO
Aida	MARIA CHIARA
Radames	NICOLA MARTINUCCI
Ramfis	BONALDO GIAIOTTI
Amonasro	SILVANO CARROLI
Conductor	NELLO SANTI
Producer	VITTORIO ROSSI
Designer	VITTORIO ROSSI
Choreography	PIETER VAN DER SLOOT
Chorus master	ALDO DANIELI

Vittorio Rossi's production ranged the chorus and crowd extras over the monumental masses anchored like spurs to the stones of the Arena, lending the performance something of the sacred tone of the oratorio. The choreography by Pieter Van der Sloot drew unreserved praise for its freshness and originality.

AIDA
1 9 9 2

King of Egypt	FRANCO DE GRANDIS
Amneris	GAIL GILMORE
Aida	SHARON SWEET
Radames	NICOLA MARTINUCCI
Ramfis	BONALDO GIAIOTTI
Amonasro	PAOLO GAVANELLI
Conductor	NELLO SANTI
Producer	GIANFRANCO DE BOSIO
Choreography	SUSANNA EGRI
Scenery	RINALDO OLIVIERI
(after sets by Ettore Fagiuoli)	
Chorus master	ALDO DANIELI

The Verona Arena has always been one of the few theatres in the world that pays attention to the physical appearance of the singers it engages, especially for Aida. With very few exceptions, singers in Aida have also been excellent actors, like soprano Maria Chiara, the magnificent Aida of recent seasons, and the Icelandic tenor Kristian Johannsson, seen here during his performance as Radames on 2nd August 1992.

Opposite, Bonaldo Giaiotti.

AIDA
1993

The novel feature of this Aida was the engagement of soprano Ghena Dimitrova to sing Amneris, a role which is usually taken by a mezzosoprano. In actual fact Verdi wrote the part for a soprano with a mezzo's extension. For the rest, and apart from the main singers, the 1993 Aida was very similar to the many productions seen in previous years. One extremely positive innovation was the presence of conductor Nello Santi, the acknowledged heir of Serafin, Votto and Molinari Pradelli.

Opposite, Dolora Zajic as Amneris.

King of Egypt	FRANCO DE GRANDIS
Amneris	GHENA DIMITROVA
Aida	MARIA DRAGONI
Radames	KRISTIAN JOHANNSSON
Ramfis	BONALDO GIAIOTTI
Amonasro	PAOLO GAVANELLI
Conductor	NELLO SANTI
Producer	GIANFRANCO DE BOSIO
Choreography	SUSANNA EGRI
Scenery	RINALDO OLIVIERI
(after sets by Ettore Fagiuoli)	
Chorus master	ARMANDO TASSO

AIDA
1 9 9 3

One of the chief ambitions of the world's tenors has always been to sing Radames at the Arena. Not that all this century's finest tenor voices have been heard in the role (indeed several great names are missing) but the many memorable interpreters of Radames include Francesco Merli, Mario Del Monaco, Carlo Bergonzi, Franco Corelli and Placido Domingo. The photographs show Bruno Beccaria (left), Placido Domingo and Daniela Longhi (centre), and Placido Domingo again (opposite) in the unaccustomed role of conductor during the performance on 6th August.

King of Egypt	FRANCO DE GRANDIS
Amneris	STEFANIA TOCZYSKA
Aida	DEBORAH VOIGT
Radames	BRUNO BECCARIA
Ramfis	BONALDO GIAIOTTI
Amonasro	JUAN PONS
Conductor	NELLO SANTI
Producer	GIANFRANCO DE BOSIO
Choreography	SUSANNA EGRI
Scenery	RINALDO OLIVIERI
(after sets by Ettore Fagiuoli)	
Chorus master	ARMANDO TASSO

OTELLO
1 9 8 2

Otello	VLADIMIR ATLANTOV
Desdemona	STEFKA EVSTATIEVA
Iago	PIERO CAPPUCCILLI
Cassio	ANTONIO BEVACQUA
Roderigo	ADRIANO SCHIAVON
Lodovico	GIANFRANCO CASARINI
Montano	ORAZIO MORI
Conductor	ZOLTAN PESKO
Producer	GIANFRANCO DE BOSIO
Choreographer	ROBERTO FASCILLA
Designer	VITTORIO ROSSI
Chorus master	CORRADO MIRANDOLA

Verdi's Otello *has taken a long time to establish itself at the Arena: just one production in the '20s and '30s, with the legendary Francesco Merli; another straight after the Second World War, with the excellent Ramon Vinay; and two recent appearances with the Russian tenor Vladimir Atlantov as Otello and first Stefka Evstatieva and then Kiri Te Kanawa (seen below with Atlantov) as Desdemona. Vittorio Rossi's scenery for the 1982 production echoed the architectural motifs of Cyprus under Venetian rule.*

Otello	Vladimir Atlantov
Desdemona	Daniela Dessì
Iago	Giorgio Zancanaro
Cassio	Jerold Siena
Roderigo	Angelo Casertano
Lodovico	Carlo Striuli
Montano	Angelo Nosotti
Conductor	Daniel Oren
Producer	Giuliano Montaldo
Scenery	Luciano Ricceri
Costumes	Elisabetta Montaldo
Choreography	Jeremy Leslie-Spinks
Chorus master	Armando Tasso

The Mexican-Spanish tenor Placido Domingo sang in two performances of Otello *at the Arena in the 1994 season. Domingo's was modelled on Ramon Vinay's Moor rather than Merli's, an intimate portrait which explored the state of mind of a character faced with his own physical and moral decline. Daniela Dessì was a wonderful Desdemona (seen right with Domingo) and Ricceri's scenery was inspired by the paintings of XV Cent. Venetian artist Vittore Carpaccio.*

The set for the 1982 Macbeth (the name of the designer does not appear on the poster) was a clear rejection of all the scenery that had been used at the Arena since 1913. The stage stretched back on two levels into the curve of the amphitheatre and relied simply on the presence of singers and chorus to evoke the settings of the drama. Villagrossi's brilliant costumes stood out to stunning effect against this earthen-coloured background.

Macbeth	RENATO BRUSON
Banquo	BONALDO GIAIOTTI
Lady Macbeth	GHENA DIMITROVA
Macduff	ERNESTO VERONELLI
Malcolm	GIANFRANCO MANGANOTTI
Murderer	GIOVANNI ANTONINI
Conductor	NELLO SANTI
Producer	RENZO GIACCHIERI
Choreography	ROBERTO FASCILLA
Costumes	FERRUCCIO VILLAGROSSI
Chorus master	CORRADO MIRANDOLA

I LOMBARDI ALLA PRIMA CROCIATA
1 9 8 4

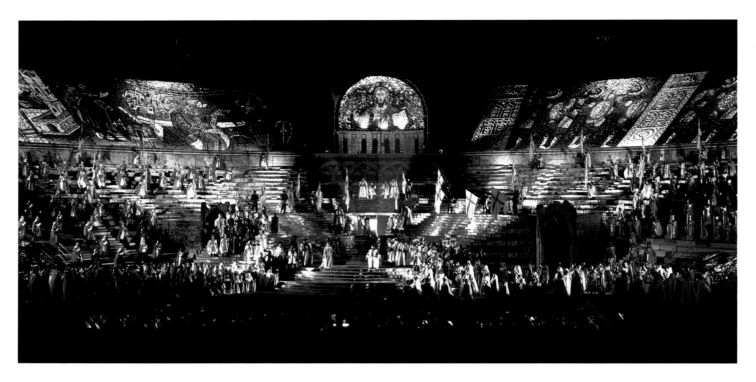

Arvino	Ezio Di Cesare
Pagano	Ruggero Raimondi
Viclinda	Fiorella Prandini
Giselda	Katia Ricciarelli
Pirro	Giorgio Surjan
The Prior of Milan	Giampaolo Corradi
Acciano	Gianfranco Casarini
Oronte	Veriano Luchetti
Sofia	Aida Meneghelli
Conductor	Maurizio Arena
Producer	Attilio Colonnello
Designer	Attilio Colonnello
Chorus master	Tullio Boni

The illustrations offer clear evidence of the producer-designer's technique of using no more than the presence of his singers and chorus to set each separate scene. One striking feature of the design was the band of mosaics placed high up around the curve behind the stage. The high point of the opera was the celebrated chorus "O Signor dal tetto natio", regularly encored at every performance.

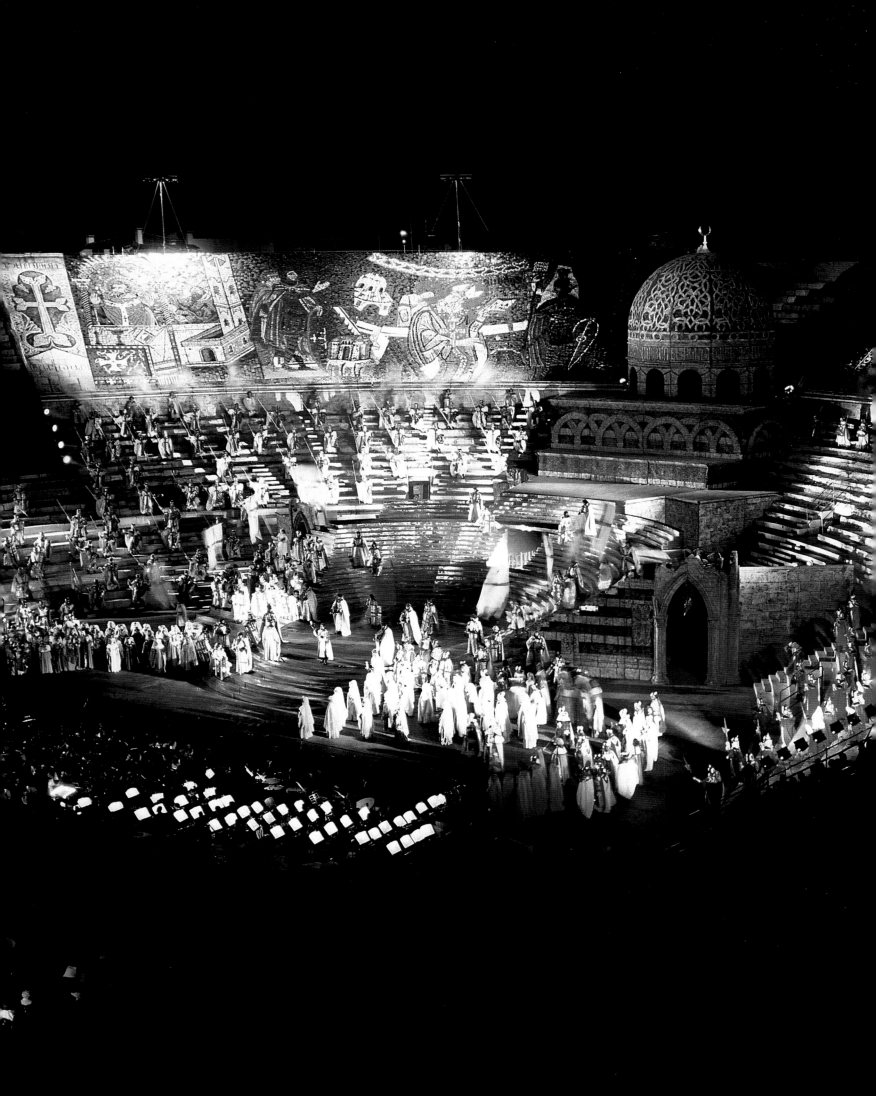

IL TROVATORE

Interest in the 1985 Il trovatore *was focussed mainly on the scenery of Mario Ceroli, the celebrated sculptor in wood. A whole armoury of pre-Renaissance and Renaissance war machines was assembled on the stage to striking effect, reminiscent of Simone Martini and Leonardo Da Vinci.*

Count di Luna	MATTEO MANUGUERRA
Leonora	ELENA MAUTI NUNZIATA
Azucena	LUDMILLA SEMCIUK
Manrico	FRANCO BONISOLLI
Ferrando	PAOLO WASHINGTON
Ines	M. GABRIELLA ONESTI
Ruiz	GIAMPAOLO CORRADI
Conductor	REYNALD GIOVANINETTI
Producer	GIUSEPPE PATRONI GRIFFI
Designer	MARIO CEROLI
Costumes	GABRIELLA PESCUCCI
Chorus master	TULLIO BONI

IL TROVATORE
1 9 8 5

LEONORA —
2° ATTO ARRIVA CONVENTO

Attila	BONALDO GIAIOTTI
Ezio	SILVANO CARROLI
Odabella	MARIA CHIARA
Foresto	VERIANO LUCHETTI
Uldino	MARIO FERRARA
Leone	GIANNI BRUNELLI
Conductor	NELLO SANTI
Producer	GIULIANO MONTALDO
Scenery	LUCIANO RICCERI
Costumes	NANÀ NECCHI
Chorus master	TULLIO BONI

The scenery designs of Luciano Ricceri set out to evoke the decadence of the Roman Empire following the first invasions of the barbarian tribes. A tree rose from the earth of the stage and held between its branches fragments of "moss-covered courtyards and crumbling forums". The photographs depict crowd scenes in the only production the Arena has so far given Attila.

UN BALLO IN MASCHERA
1 9 8 6

Riccardo	LUIS LIMA
Renato	SILVANO CARROLI
Amelia	MARIA CHIARA
Ulrica	GAIL GILMORE
Oscar	ALIDA FERRARINI
Silvano	ALBERTO NOLI
Samuel	MARIO RINAUDO
Conductor	GUSTAV KUHN
Producer	PIETRO ZUFFI
Designer	PIETRO ZUFFI
Choreography	MARIO PISTONI
Chorus master	ALDO DANIELI

Apart from the musical talents of the singers and Gustav Kuhn the conductor, the 1986 Ballo *was most notable for the set which Pietro Zuffi created for the last act, where, after a scene played out in the semi-darkness of an interior room, the façade of a Renaissance palazzo is suddenly flooded with light.*

UN BALLO IN MASCHERA
1 9 8 6

Violetta Valéry	Nelly Miricioiu
Flora Bervoix	Aida Meneghelli
Annina	Marisa Zotti
Alfredo Germont	Franco Bonisolli
Giorgio Germont	Giorgio Zancanaro
Gastone	Gianfranco Manganotti
Doctor Grenvil	Giovanni Furlanetto
Conductor	Ralf Weikert
Producer	Gianfranco De Bosio
Scenery	Nicola Rubertelli
Choreography	Roberto Fascilla
Costumes	Zaira De Vincentiis
Chorus master	Aldo Danieli

The scenery and costumes of this 1987 production of La traviata *shift the action of the play by Alexandre Dumas* fils *into the early years of the XX Cent., a decade or so later than the time Visconti chose for his La Scala version with Maria Callas on 28th May 1955.*

Below, Julia Conwell.

LA TRAVIATA
1 9 8 7

Violetta Valéry	DANIELA LONGHI
Flora Bervoix	MONICA MINARELLI
Annina	BERNADETTE LUCARINI
Alfredo Germont	SALVATORE FISICHELLA
Giorgio Germont	RENATO BRUSON
Gastone	ALDO BOTTION
Doctor Genvil	GIANCARLO BOLDRINI
Conductor	GUSTAV KUHN
Producer	LUCIANO DAMIANI
Scenery	LUCIANO DAMIANI
Costumes	SYBILLE ULSAMER
Choreography	JEREMY LESLIE-SPINKS
Chorus master	ARMANDO TASSO

The 1993 La traviata *is remembered chiefly for Luciano Damiano's set designs, the effect of which was a series of immense paintings stretching across the width of the arena stage. Sybille Ulsamer's costumes were highly praised but Damiano's production provoked considerable criticism.*

Nabucco	SILVANO CARROLI
Ismaele	GIORGIO TIEPPO
Zaccaria	PAATA BURCHULADZE
Abigaille	LINDA ROARK STRUMMER
Fenena	MARTHA SENN
High Priest of Baal	FRANCO FEDERICI
Abdallo	ALDO BOTTION
Anna	ELENA ANGELI
Conductor	DANIEL OREN
Producer	VITTORIO ROSSI
Designer	VITTORIO ROSSI
Chorus master	ALDO DANIELI

Nabucco *has come into its own at the Arena only during the last decade, thanks to excellent singers, designers, producers and conductors. The part of Zaccaria was shared by Paata Burchuladze, Bonaldo Giaiotti and Yevgeny Nestorenko (the latter singers are seen bottom left and right respectively).*

NABUCCO
1 9 8 9

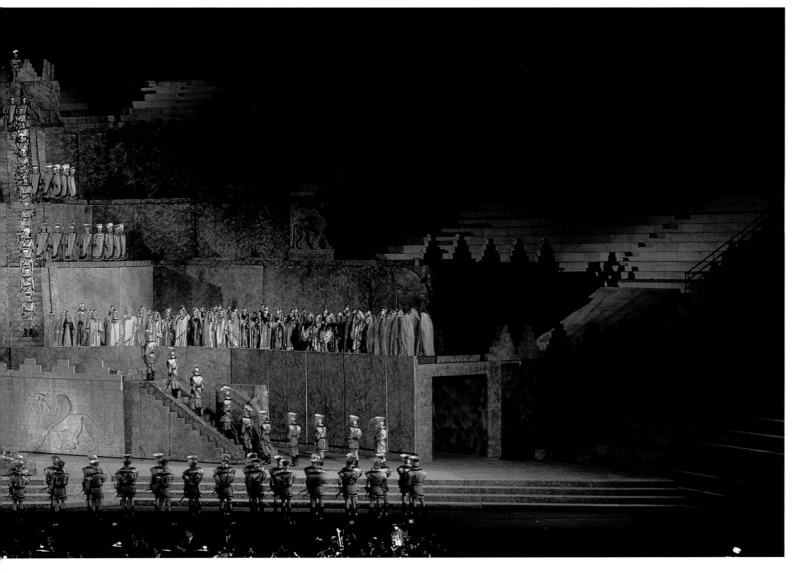

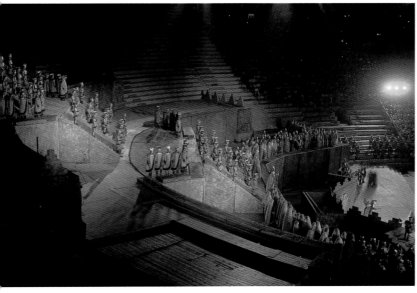

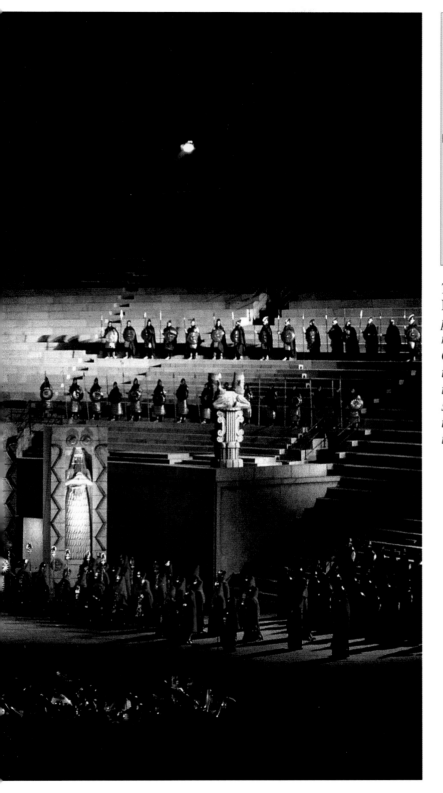

1991	
Nabucco	PIERO CAPPUCCILLI
Ismaele	NUNZIO TODISCO
Zaccaria	YEVGENY NESTERENKO
Abigaille	GHENA DIMITROVA
Fenena	STEFKA MINEVA
High Priest of Baal	CARLO STRIULI
Abdallo	ANGELO CASERTANO
Anna	MINA BLUM
Conductor	DANIEL OREN
Producer	GIANFRANCO DE BOSIO
Scenery	RINALDO OLIVIERI
Costumes	PASQUALE GROSSI
Chorus master	ALDO DANIELI

1992	
Nabucco	PIERO CAPPUCCILLI
Ismaele	NUNZIO TODISCO
Zaccaria	ROBERTO SCANDIUZZI
Abigaille	LINDA ROARK STRUMMER
Fenena	MARTHA SENN
High Priest of Baal	CARLO DEL BOSCO
Abdallo	ALDO BOTTION
Anna	COSETTA TOSETTI
Conductor	ANTON GUADAGNO
Producer	GIANFRANCO DE BOSIO
Scenery	RINALDO OLIVIERI
Costumes	PASQUALE GROSSI
Chorus master	ALDO DANIELI

The 1991, 1992 and 1994 Nabucco *was unanimously praised by the critics as a model for future productions. Overwhelming enthusiasm too for the famous Chorus of the Hebrew Slaves, with the singers spreading out among the audience for the inevitable encores.*

NABUCCO
1994

Nabucco	RENATO BRUSON
Ismaele	GILBERTO MAFFEZZONI
Zaccaria	BONALDO GIAIOTTI
Abigaille	MONICA PICK-HIERONIMI
Fenena	ANNA SCHIATTI
High Priest of Baal	CARLO DEL BOSCO
Abdallo	OSLAVIO DI CREDICO
Anna	MINA BLUM
Conductor	JAN LATHAN-KOENIG
Producer	GIANFRANCO DE BOSIO
Scenery	RINALDO OLIVIERI
Costumes	PASQUALE GROSSI
Chorus master	ARMANDO TASSO

The scenery for the 1994 Nabucco was designed specifically for producer De Bosio, who arranged his choral forces on the stage and extras on the banked terraces behind them with memorable pictorial and plastic effect. The cast made admirable efforts to lend credibility to characters that are more symbols than real human beings. In the photograph, Monica Pick-Hieronimi.

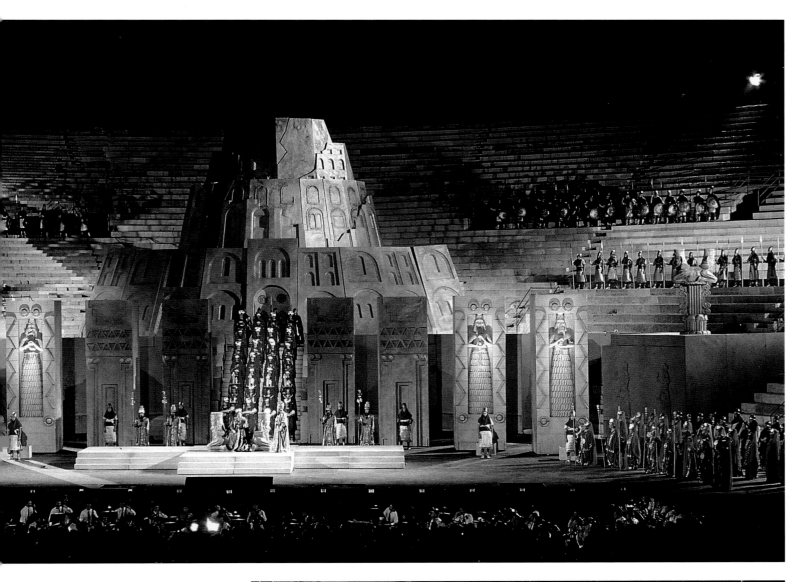

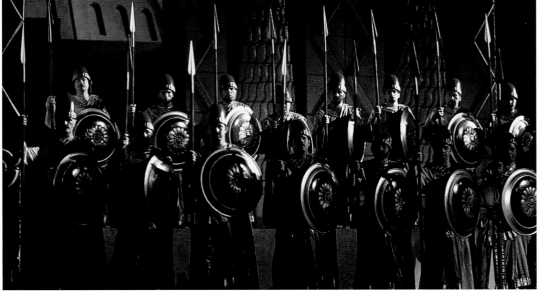

LA FORZA DEL DESTINO

1 9 8 9

Marchese	FILIPPO MILITANO
Donna Leonora	MARIA CHIARA
Don Carlos	GIORGIO ZANCANARO
Don Alvaro	GIUSEPPE GIACOMINI
Preziosilla	BRUNA BAGLIONI
Padre Guardiano	BONALDO GIAIOTTI
Fra' Melitone	GIAMPIERO MASTROMEI
Curra	SERENA PASQUALINI
Conductor	ALEXANDER LAZAREV
Producer	SANDRO BOLCHI
Scenery	GIANFRANCO PADOVANI
Choreography	BRUNO MALUSÀ
Chorus master	ALDO DANIELI

La forza del destino *is one of the best-loved and most frequently presented of Arena operas, and the 1989 production engaged an excellent cast of singers under Alexander Lazarev as conductor and Sandro Bolchi as producer, with impressive and effective scenery designed by Gianfranco Padovani. In the photograph, Bruna Baglioni and Giorgio Zancanaro.*

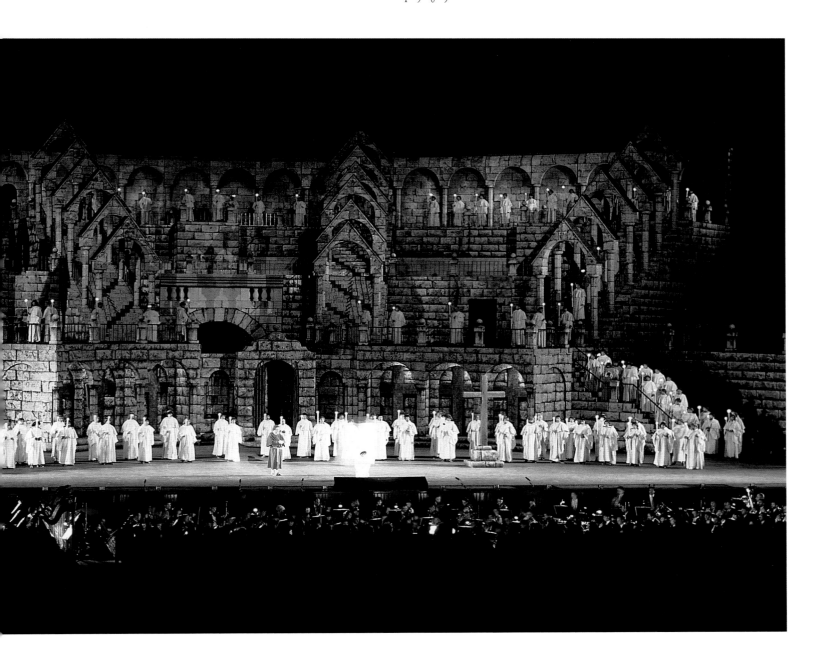

MESSA DA REQUIEM
1990

Luciano Pavarotti is the latest in the distinguished line of undisputed stars of the international opera stage, including Beniamino Gigli, Giacomo Lauri Volpi, Francesco Merli and Tito Schipa, whose very presence arouses unbounded excitement and expectation.

After the triumphs of La Gioconda, Un ballo in maschera *and* Il trovatore, *Pavarotti returned to the Arena to sing in Verdi's* Requiem *in 1990.*

Below, left to right, Sharon Sweet, Dolora Zajic, Lorin Maazel, Luciano Pavarotti and Paul Plishka.

Conductor	LORIN MAAZEL
Soprano	SHARON SWEET
Mezzosoprano	DOLORA ZAJIC
Tenor	LUCIANO PAVAROTTI
Bass	PAUL PLISHKA
Orchestra	MOSCOW PHILHARMONIC
Choir	THE WORLD FESTIVAL
Chorus master	JAN JENSEN

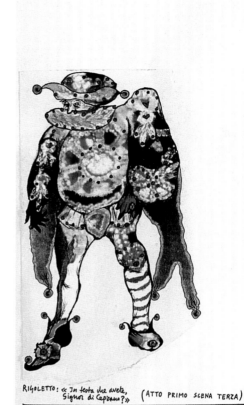

RIGOLETTO
VERDI
ARENA
VERONA
1991
REGIA
SCENE
COSTUMI
SYLVANO
BUSSOTTI

RIGOLETTO: « In testa che avete, Signor di Ceprano?» (ATTO PRIMO SCENA TERZA)

Duke of Mantua	MARCELLO GIORDANI
Rigoletto	LEO NUCCI
Gilda	MARIELLA DEVIA
Sparafucile	MIKHAIL RYSSOV
Maddalena	SERENA LAZZARINI
Count Monterone	DANILO RIGOSA
Giovanna	LUCIA MASSARI
Marullo	ANDREA PICCINNI
Conductor	RICO SACCANI
Producer	SYLVANO BUSSOTTI
Designer	SYLVANO BUSSOTTI
Choreography	ROCCO
Chorus master	ALDO DANIELI

Like Il trovatore *and* La traviata, Rigoletto *is one of those operas that seems to provoke fervent discussion and controversy after every performance. The 1991 Arena production was certainly no exception, audiences and the critics managing to agree only about Devia's Gilda. Nucci gave a remarkably involved and involving performance as Rigoletto.*

Opposite, Luciana Palombi as the Countess Ceprano and Marcello Giordani as the Duke of Mantua.

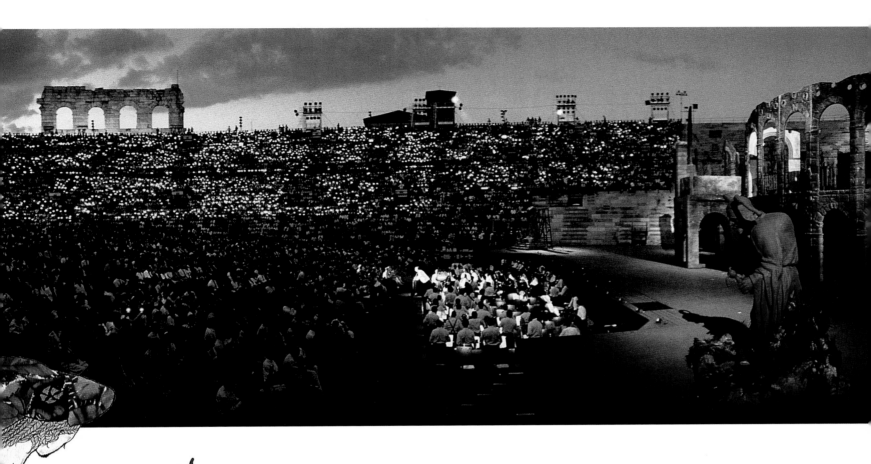

DON CARLO
1 9 9 2

Philip II	ROBERTO SCANDIUZZI
Don Carlo	ALBERTO CUPIDO
Rodrigo	RENATO BRUSON
Grand Inquisitor	KURT RYDL
A Friar	ARMANDO CAFORIO
Elisabeth de Valois	APRILE MILLO
Princess Eboli	GIOVANNA CASOLLA
Tebaldo	DANIELA BENORI
Conductor	GUSTAV KUHN
Producer	RENZO GIACCHIERI
Scenery	DANTE FERRETTI
Costumes	GABRIELLA PESCUCCI
Chorus master	ALDO DANIELI

It was perhaps inevitable that the 1992 Don Carlo *should suffer by comparison with the "historic" 1969 production: the latest version had an excellent cast, including Bruson (seen right), and a great conductor in Kuhn, but the production and scenery played too much on references to Baroque painting while failing to capture its tragic spirit.*

THE OPERAS OF GIACOMO PUCCINI

The presence of Giacomo Puccini at the Arena raises far more complex problems than would appear from a summary glance at lists of the productions his operas have received there. To state that Puccini and his works represent an Italy, a taste and an aesthetic concept which are the direct opposite of those we identify with Verdi may going a bit far, but they are certainly very different. Puccini's *Manon Lescaut* and Verdi's *Falstaff* are chronologically close but at the same time a whole world apart. Verdi was the artist of the Risorgimento, whereas Puccini paid no attention to politics and still less did he worry about the moral and civil regeneration of the Italian nation. He grew up and flourished artistically in the period of King Umberto I and then of Prime Minister Giolitti and against a background of quite different priorities. Before bothering about external events Puccini focused on the workings of the human heart and soul. The worldwide success of his operas arises first from the music, of course, but also from the fact that every member of the audience can identify emotionally with the characters on stage. Puccini was born in Lucca in 1858 and died in Brussels in 1924; he inherited a strong musical tradition from his family, but whereas they had written and performed for the church, Giacomo concentrated solely on opera. He was taught by Ponchielli at the Conservatoire in Milan and made his debut with *Le Villi*, followed by the semi-success of *Edgar*.

His first international success came in Turin in 1893 with *Manon Lescaut*, with its already distinctive, warm, melodic vein and remarkable command of instrumentation. Thereafter there was a Puccini première almost every three years and they regularly conformed to a pattern of a controversial first night followed by a string of successful performances in Italy and abroad. Thus *La Bohème* with its nostalgic recreation of Paris in the 1830s, and *Tosca* with its magnificent evocation of papal Rome in the turbulent period following the French Revolution. The fiasco of *Madama Butterfly* at La Scala in Milan and its triumphant comeback shortly afterwards in Brescia marked the break between Puccini and a certain sort of Italian musical culture. *La fanciulla del West* enjoyed a rapturous reception, but at the Metropolitan in New York. Then followed *Il trittico*, the moderately successful *La Rondine* and the long gestation of *Turandot*, interrupted by illness and finally left unfinished. Puccini was in the audience at the 1913 Arena *Aida*. He spoke glowingly of the experience but refrained from any

speculation about whether his own work might also be
presented in the immense space of the amphitheatre.
It was only after the posthumous première of *Turandot* at La
Scala in 1926 that plans began to be made for it to be
performed at the Arena. Only *Turandot* however, for all the
other operas were considered too intimate to lend
themselves to effective productions in the open air. Though
opinions in this respect did change, the ten seasons and 75
performances of *Turandot* make it the most frequently seen
of Puccini's operas at the Arena. As well as offering
wonderful opportunities for striking scenery and exciting
writing for massed choruses and a huge orchestra, *Turandot*
also demands great singers; and the Arena met the challenge

by making the opera a showcase for some of the century's
finest, from Lauri Volpi to Corelli and from Domingo to
Martinucci in the part of Calaf, while the Icy Princess and
the slave-girl Liù have been sung by a succession of
distinguished sopranos including Cigna, Favero, Nilsson,
Olivero, and more recently Ghena Dimitrova and Cecilia
Gasdia. The more recent productions of *Turandot* (1983 -
1988) have tended to concentrate attention less on the
voices than on the fantastical scenery of Luciano Ricceri

and Serge Creuz or the original and resourceful productions of Giuliano Montaldo and Raymond Rossius.

The one truly memorable *Turandot* came in 1969 when an awe-inspiring Birgit Nilsson sang with the brilliant young Placido Domingo and Pier Luigi Pizzi's silvery Peking against the deep blue night sky provided a backdrop which was the visual correlative of the colours Francesco Molinari Pradelli and his orchestra drew from Puccini's score.

La Bohème entered the Arena thanks to great singers being prepared to don heavy winter costumes on sweltering Summer nights for the privilege of singing Puccini's masterpiece there. The Arena's first Rodolfo was the acclaimed Giuseppe Lugo, and his successors have included Giuseppe Di Stefano, Gianni Raimondi, Luciano Pavarotti and the most recent, Neil Shicoff. Their Mimìs have ranged superbly from Mafalda Favero to Rina Gigli, Renata Scotto and Cecilia Gasdia. Once *Tosca* was introduced to the Arena (by Giuseppe Lugo again) it immediately joined *Aida* as a quintessentially "Arena" opera: hardly surprising given the combination of three spectacular settings - Sant'Andrea della Valle, Palazzo Farnese and Castel Sant'Angelo - and instantly memorable music such as the powerful "Te Deum" that concludes Act I and the wonderfully atmospheric dawn breaking over Rome in Act III, not to mention arias which, when well sung, will defy any audience not to leap to its

The Arena in Verona, like La Scala in Milan and the Olimpico in Vicenza, is a theatre where the audience itself provides part of the theatrical experience. One fanciful critic wrote that the crowded tiers banked around the arena conjured images of the "candida rosa" of Dante's Paradiso. Here the audience has filled the Arena right to the topmost row of seats perched on the outer wall of the amphitheatre, still astonishingly in place after almost two thousand years of exposure to earthquakes and removal of the monument's masonry.

feet and demand an encore. Two tigresses of the opera stage, Gina Cigna and Maria Caniglia, sang Tosca to Lugo's Cavaradossi, and later Giuseppe Di Stefano and Franco Corelli were partnered by the finest Tosca of all time, the consummate actress and unforgettable singer Magda Olivero. The Arena has heard many magnificent Baron Scarpias too, but none so distinguished as Tito Gobbi, who managed somehow to remain a gentleman even when playing a chauvinist libertine dealing with a singer who is in love with another. In attempting to emulate the success of previous productions the latest *Tosca* (1990) banked on the inspired and dynamic conducting of Daniel Oren and the mature interpretations of Giovanna Casolla and Alberto Cupido. The production was by Luigi Squarzina.

The history of *Madama Butterfly* at the Arena is quite different, only two productions having been seen there and those quite recently (1983 and 1987). The opera has always been a firm favourite with Puccini fans, though it has often taken a battering from the critics not so much for its orchestral and vocal components (which rank indeed amongst the composer's finest achievements) as for the

sugary sentimentality of the story. In more recent times, producers have attempted to shift the focus and concentrate on the collapse of the American dream and the way the clash of two civilizations leads to the inevitable capitulation of the older. The delay in the opera's arrival at the Arena was due to the general conviction that *Madama Butterfly* was unsuitable because it is mainly intimate in character, with arias, duets and trios but no great choral music. All perfectly true, but such a view ignores the compensating fact that Cio-Cio-San dominates the opera like the heroine of a classical tragedy and is present on stage from almost beginning to end. The decision to put on an opera like *Butterfly* is justified only if a great singer-actress can be engaged for the part (Mafalda Favero, Rosetta Pampanini, Renata Tebaldi, Maria Callas or Magda Olivero could all have been memorable Arena Butterflies, perhaps offsetting some of the more dubious cultural choices of yesteryear). Fortunately the Arena hastened to make good all those years of neglect when it found an ideal Cio-Cio-San in Raina Kabaivanska. Not that Kabaivanska possesses the paradisiacal timbre that our nineteenth century ancestors so prized, but she is perhaps the last in the line of superb singer-actresses who have graced the Italian stage, starting with Gemma Bellincioni and Lina Cavalieri and continuing with Iva Pacetti, Claudia Muzio and Magda Olivero. So until we see another Kabaivanska it is better that *Madama Butterfly* should keep its distance from the Arena.

Similar comments might be made about *Manon Lescaut*, which has so far been seen only once. But in that one season Magda Olivero and Placido Domingo gloriously made up for all the lost years and the applause at the end of the opera lasted longer than the whole of the last act. Though not a frequent visitor, *La fanciulla del West* is at least judged an ideal opera for presentation at the Arena, not so much for its setting among the mountains and woods of California as for the rich orchestration. First produced at the Arena in 1949, *La fanciulla* had to wait until 1960 for the perfect performance, from a trio of singers of the kind Superintendents can now only dream of: Magda Olivero, Franco Corelli and Giangiacomo Guelfi. Revived in 1986, the opera was well received, but never with the incandescent enthusiasm it had kindled a quarter of a century earlier. Space has not so far been found for *Il Trittico*, but it is not out of the question that the three one-act operas may one day be heard at the Arena, perhaps separately in programmes with works by other composers.

LA BOHEME
1982

Rodolfo	PETER DVORSKY
Mimì	RAINA KABAIVANSKA
Marcello	GARBIS BOYAGIAN
Schaunard	ROBERTO COVIELLO
Colline	PAOLO WASHINGTON
Benoît	GIUSEPPE ZECCHILLO
Alcindoro	GRAZIANO POLIDORI
Musetta	PAMELA KUCENIC
Conductor	ANTON GUADAGNO
Producer	DARIO DALLA CORTE
Scenery	ANTONIO MASTROMATTEI
Costumes	PIER LUCIANO CAVALLOTTI
Chorus master	CORRADO MIRANDOLA

Antonio Mastromattei's sets solved the difficult problem of how to reconcile La Bohème *and the Arena with a view of the roofs of Paris forming a background to the humble attic studio, which revolved to become the Café Momus and the Barrière d'Enfer.*

LA BOHEME
1992

Rodolfo	VINCENZO LA SCOLA
Mimì	LUCIA MAZZARIA
Marcello	ANGELO VECCIA
Schaunard	ORAZIO MORI
Colline	CARLO COLOMBARA
Benoît	GRAZIANO POLIDORI
Alcindoro	GIUSEPPE RIVA
Musetta	SANDRA PACETTI
Conductor	TIZIANO SEVERINI
Producer	GIULIANO MONTALDO
Scenery	LUCIANO RICCERI
Costumes	ELISABETTA MONTALDO
Chorus master	ALDO DANIELI

In 1992 and 1994 La Bohème *was given the splendid designs of Luciano Ricceri and a masterly production by Giuliano Montaldo. In the setting of Paris in the 1830s, the four bohèmiens,* Mimì and Musetta *elegantly recreated exactly the atmosphere Puccini had in mind for an opera which still marks one of the high points in the history of Italian opera.*

LA BOHÈME
1994

Rodolfo	ALBERTO CUPIDO
Mimì	CECILIA GASDIA
Marcello	ALESSANDRO CORBELLI
Schaunard	ROBERTO DE CANDIA
Colline	GIORGIO SURJAN
Benoît	GRAZIANO POLIDORI
Alcindoro	ANDREA SNARSKY
Musetta	MARQUITA LISTER
Conductor	ROBERTO TOLOMELLI
Producer	GIULIANO MONTALDO
Scenery	LUCIANO RICCERI
Costumes	ELISABETTA MONTALDO
Chorus master	ARMANDO TASSO

For his production of La Bohème *in 1992 and 1994, Giuliano Montaldo had an unforgettable Mimì in Cecilia Gasdia (seen opposite with Placido Domingo) and two generous Rodolfos in Neil Shicoff and Alberto Cupido. One of the factors that made the production so popular was the sense it gave of full involvement with the story, a well-remembered characteristic of Arena productions of the 1950s, a period which was also rich in particularly fine singers.*

LA BOHEME
1 9 9 4

TURANDOT
1 9 8 3

Turandot	GHENA DIMITROVA
Emperor Altoum	GIAMPAOLO CORRADI
Timur	FERRUCCIO FURLANETTO
Calaf	NICOLA MARTINUCCI
Liù	CECILIA GASDIA
Ping	GRAZIANO POLIDORI
Pang	PIER FRANCESCO POLI
Pong	ANTONIO BEVACQUA
Conductor	MAURIZIO ARENA
Producer	GIULIANO MONTALDO
Scenery	LUCIANO RICCERI
Costumes	NANÀ CECCHI
Choreograpy	HAL JAMANOUCHI
Chorus master	CORRADO MIRANDOLA

The television series Marco Polo *exerted a certain influence over the choice of Giuliano Montaldo as producer of the 1983* Turandot.
Luciano Ricceri's sets were reminiscent of the Forbidden City in Peking, with the great curve of the Arena as if frescoed in blue, the tops of the imperial palaces lost among the clouds of the sky.

TURANDOT
1988

Scenery and costumes for the 1988 Turandot *were designed by Serge Creuz, and the producer was Raymond Rossius. While the intention of Puccini was to give Carlo Gozzi's fable the force of credibility, Creuz and Rossius were intent on pushing the story of the Icy Princess towards the absurd, the fantastic, the unreal. The effect of the scenery was of a reinvented China rather than a copy or imitation.*

Opposite, Ghena Dimitrova as Turandot.

Turandot	GHENA DIMITROVA
Emperor Altoum	ANGELO CASERTANO
Timur	ROBERTO SCANDIUZZI
Calaf	NICOLA MARTINUCCI
Liù	ALIDA FERRARINI
Ping	ORAZIO MORI
Pang	OSLAVIO DI CREDICO
Pong	PIERO DE PALMA
Conductor	DANIEL OREN
Producer	RAYMOND ROSSIUS
Designer	SERGE CREUZ
Chorus master	ALDO DANIELI

Turandot	GRACE BUMBRY
Emperor Altoum	MARIO GUGGIA
Timur	CARLO STRIULI
Calaf	KRISTIAN JOHANNSSON
Liù	MIETTA SIGHELE
Ping	ALFONSO ANTONIOZZI
Pang	SERGIO BERTOCCHI
Pong	JORIO ZENNARO
Conductor	DANIEL NAZARETH
Producer	GIULIANO MONTALDO
Scenery	LUCIANO RICCERI
Costumes	ELISABETTA MONTALDO
Chorus master	ALDO DANIELI

The 1991 Turandot *was a revival of Giuliano Montaldo's 1983 production, designed by Luciano Ricceri. The general impression was of a return to order after the unrestrained fantasies of Rossius, and of firm reference to the ideas of Puccini, Adami and Simoni. The Riddle Scene made its customary powerful effect, but the singers were unimpressive by comparison with the stars of yesteryear.*

Madama Butterfly
in the Arena means
Raina Kabaivanska, whose
Cio-Cio-San approaches the
stature of the heroine in a
Greek tragedy.
Unfortunately the Italian
opera scene seems no
longer to be producing
actress-singers in the mould
of Claudia Muzio and
Gemma Bellincioni, Maria
Callas and Magda Olivero;
there are fine singers, of
course, some perhaps with
more beautiful voices than
Kabaivanska's, but very few
are capable of truly moving
an audience, of compelling
utter involvement in the
story of the Japanese geisha
girl. Giulio Chazalettes
provided a model
production and
Ulisse Santecchi elegant,
realistic set designs.

MADAMA BUTTERFLY
1 9 8 3

Butterfly	RAINA KABAIVANSKA
Suzuki	ELEONORA JANKOVIC
Kate Pinkerton	MARISA ZOTTI
F.B. Pinkerton	NAZZARENO ANTINORI
Sharpless	LORENZO SACCOMANI
Goro	MARIO FERRARA
Prince Yamadori	GIUSEPPE ZECCHILLO
The bonze	GIANNI BRUNELLI
Conductor	MAURIZIO ARENA
Producer	GIULIO CHAZALETTES
Designer	ULISSE SANTICCHI
Chorus master	CORRADO MIRANDOLA

MADAMA BUTTERFLY
1987

Butterfly	MIETTA SIGHELE
Suzuki	ELEONORA JANKOVIC
Kate Pinkerton	IVANA TURCHESE
F.B. Pinkerton	VERIANO LUCHETTI
Sharpless	ALBERTO RINALDI
Goro	MARIO GUGGIA
Prince Yamadori	ALBERTO CARUSI
Conductor	YOSHINORI KIKUCHI
Producer	RENATA SCOTTO
Costumes	RENATA SCOTTO
Scenery	FERRUCCIO VILLAGROSSI
Chorus master	ALDO DANIELI

One of the performances of the 1987 Butterfly was sung by Renata Scotto, who also produced the opera that year. Scotto's voice was reminiscent of that of Rosina Storchio, the first lyric soprano to sing Cio-Cio-San, before Kruceniski headed the line of dramatic sopranos who sang the part. Apart from Scotto's one performance, Butterfly was sung by Mietta Sighele (seen left). The scenery was designed by Ferruccio Villagrossi.

TOSCA
1984

Floria Tosca	SHIRLEY VERRETT
Cavaradossi	GIACOMO ARAGALL
Baron Scarpia	SILVANO CARROLI
Cesare Angelotti	ALFREDO GIACOMOTTI
Sacristan	GRAZIANO POLIDORI
Spoletta	MARIO FERRARA
Sciarrone	BRUNO GRELLA
A gaoler	GIANNI BRUNELLI
Conductor	DANIEL OREN
Producer	SYLVANO BUSSOTTI
Scenery	FIORENZO GIORGI
Chorus master	TULLIO BONI

In the 1984 Tosca, *designer Fiorenzo Giorgi's intended evocation of Roman Baroque through a single striking image did not come off: Bernini's* Gloria, *a column of a baldaquin beside the Trevi Fountain and sundry other details failed to establish an appropriate atmosphere for Puccini's* Tosca, *though this was certainly present through Daniel Oren's conducting and the performances of several of the singers, including Giacomo Aragall, Giampiero Mastromei and Ingvar Wixell (seen above with Eva Marton).*

Floria Tosca	GIOVANNA CASOLLA
Cavaradossi	ALBERTO CUPIDO
Baron Scarpia	SILVANO CARROLI
Cesare Angelotti	FRANCO FEDERICI
Sacristan	ALFREDO MARIOTTI
Spoletta	ANGELO CASERTANO
Sciarrone	ALBERTO CARUSI
A gaoler	ANDREA PICCINNI
Conductor	DANIEL OREN
Producer	LUIGI SQUARZINA
Designer	GIOVANNI AGOSTINUCCI
Chorus master	ALDO DANIELI

For the 1990 production, Giovanni Agostinucci attempted to convey the essence of Roman Baroque with a fanciful staircase, which in truth would have looked more appropriate in a garden than in Sant'Andrea della Valle; his set for the Castel Sant'Angelo scene was more convincing. Daniel Oren again provided distinguished conducting, and Luigi Squarzina an unremarkable but attentive production.

Opposite, Giovanna Casolla and Silvano Carroli.

TOSCA
1 9 9 0

LA FANCIULLA DEL WEST
1 9 8 6

For the 1986 production of Puccini's "American" opera it was clear that suitable Italian voices were simply not available: Minnie and Dick Johnson had to be sought in America and Russia. Production and scenery aroused little enthusiasm.

Below, Sofia Larson as Minnie.

Minnie	SOFIA LARSON
Jack Rance	SILVANO CARROLI
Dick Johnson	VLADIMIR POPOV
Nick	FLORINDO ANDREOLLI
Ashby	CARLO DEL BOSCO
Sonora	GIOVANNI DE ANGELIS
Trin	FRANCESCO MEMEO
Sid	GIUSEPPE ZECCHILLO
Conductor	MAURIZIO ARENA
Producer	EZIO ZEFFERI
Scenery	LUCIANO RICCERI
Costumes	GIANNI AND TITTI FIORE
Chorus master	ALDO DANIELI

LA FANCIULLA DEL WEST

1 9 8 6

THE OTHER OPERAS

One of the problems facing the Arena management from the beginning was how to repeat the stunning success now known to be feasible with *Aida* without repeating the same opera. For the following year, perhaps to please the mezzosoprano Maria Gay Zanatello, the wife of tenor Giovanni Zenatello, it was decided to produce *Carmen*. At first sight the choice was obviously a happy one and *Carmen* duly became and has remained an Arena favourite. But behind the decision lay not only the need to satisfy a famous singer's craving to don the flounced skirts of the fiery *femme fatale*; the big question exercising the opera world in the earlier part of the

century was whether the Italian repertoire should be extended to include the German or the French opera traditions. The opera-going public obviously favoured the French, while the critics prefered the German. As it turned out, the Arena proved able to satisfy both, incorporating French operas first, and opening up to German works when the Great War was over and anti-German feeling had died down. Clearly the "Italian" *Carmen* (which incidentally was also much liked by Nietzsche) retained little connection with the Opéra Comique from which had originated: it was tragic in mood and closely related to the *verista* mode that then held sway on the Italian stage. Judging by the scanty documentary material available, the 1914 *Carmen*, with Gay Zenatello, tenor Famadas Amador and baritone Viglione Borghese, must have exemplified the characteristics of the young Italian school, with passion and vindictive fury much to the fore. *Carmen* was better served after the Second World War, with Franco Corelli a distinguished José and Giulietta Simionato a vivacious Carmen. Recent productions have placed increasing emphasis on the spectacular and have attracted crowds on a similar scale to *Aida* and *Nabucco*; indeed, Bizet's opera is still so alive and well that for once the Arena has even risked breaking its self-imposed Italian-only rule and given it in French.

The only concession to popular taste in Arena productions of *Carmen* is their incorporation of ballet, using incidental music that Bizet composed for Daudet's *L'Arlesienne*. Notable ballet companies engaged for this purpose have included those of Pilar Lopez (1961), Luisillo (1965) and most recently the company directed by El Camborio and Lucia Real. It's difficult to understand why, but the Arena seems more interested in the tenor and soprano in the roles of José and Micaëla than in the mezzosoprano who sings Carmen. Memorable renditions of José have come from Corelli, the Chilean tenor Ramon Vinay and the Spaniard José Carreras, while Renata Scotto and Mirella Freni (in her only appearance at the Arena) have given affecting portraits of Micaëla.

As we mentioned earlier, the modern tradition of opera at the Arena began when *verismo* was all the rage, so as one would expect, all the operas rightly or wrongly perceived as *veriste* sooner or later made their appearance in the amphitheatre. First in the line of those improperly seen in this light was Umberto Giordano's *Andrea Chénier*, which immediately enjoyed tremendous success in 1924. The imagination and enthusiasm of Italian opera-goers were still kindled by the French Revolution and its heroes, and even more so by the powerfully expansive and impetuous music of the passionate southerner Giordano. The Arena understood that the trump card for *Andrea Chénier*, inevitably subjected to comparison with the cornerstone operas of the Italian tradition, was to ensure that its romances, the unfailing way to the Italian opera-lover's heart, were sung by the greatest singers of the day. Outstanding Chèniers have included Francesco Merli (1924), Beniamino Gigli (1934), Mario Del Monaco (1951), Amedeo Zambon (1967) and José Carreras (1986), while among the famous sopranos who have sung Maddalena are Maria Caniglia, Orianna Santuncone and, most recently, Monserrat Caballé; and not to forget the baritones, Benvenuto Franci, Giangiacomo Guelfi and Piero Cappuccilli.

The epitome of the Italian *verista* opera, of course, is *Cavalleria rusticana*, and it has always been treated with considerable respect at the Arena; a glance at the 1935 poster, with Lina Bruna Rasa, Galliano Masini and Carlo Tagliabue singing under the baton of the great Gino Marinuzzi, shows just how much. Then there was the exceptional revival of 1952, with the unforgettable Mario Del Monaco offering a confidently swaggering Turiddu loved by Santuzza (Elena Nicolai) and Lola (Anna Maria Canali). Giulietta Simionato gave a splendid Santuzza in 1960, with Ettore Bastianini a sternly unforgiving Alfio and Fiorenza Cossotto in the unrewarding part of Lola. Cossotto was finally given a crack at Santuzza in 1967, beside the ardent Turiddu of Gianfranco Cecchele. Stars in other highly successful revivals have included Antonietta Stella, Carlo Bergonzi and Giangiacomo Guelfi, and in 1977 Placido Domingo brought off the difficult feat of singing Turiddu in *Cavalleria* and Canio in *I pagliacci* on the same evening. The most recent production had Fiorenza Cossotto again as Santuzza, Nicola Martinucci as Turridu and Silvano Carroli as Alfio. As well as these "popular" operas, the Arena has delighted critics and connoisseur opera-lovers alike with numerous productions of culturally more demanding works. And if Borodin's *Prince Igor*, Richard Strauss's *Elektra* and *Salome* and Wagner's *Tristan und Isolde* are all still waiting to make their debut at the Arena, their time will surely come.

In the meantime, *Samson et Dalila* by Saint-Saëns was seen in 1921 and 1974, and Mussorgski's *Boris Godunov* has had three outings, of which the 1952 production was one of the all-time Arena highlights. It may not be easy to transport *Aida* audiences from the Arena to Ancient Egypt, with its sphinxes, pyramids and obelisks, but it is still more difficult to transform the stone ellipse of the amphitheatre into the Kremlin in Moscow, a monastery cell, the interior of an inn, a snow-covered forest with a blazing city in the background. But that directorial wizard Nicola Benois was utterly unfazed by the task and at the beginning of each scene his gates of St. Petersburg opened on a further stage in the tragic decline, from coronation to death, of Nicola Rossi Lemeni's prodigious Czar Boris.

A yawing gulf separates *Boris* from Amilcare Ponchielli's *La Gioconda*, an opera the Arena seems unable to do without. And whereas the Russian masterpiece has appeared three times, the story of the blonde Venetian singer has received nine productions. The critics may have been systematically demolishing *La Gioconda* for a hundred years now, but it only needs a dramatic soprano with good acting ability and the resulting success or even triumph gives the opera renewed credibility until the next time. Before and during the Second World War, Gina Cigna took inalienable possession of the part of *La Gioconda*. Then in 1947 Maria Callas made her Arena debut in the part, finding and conveying depths of passion that were beyond any other interpreter before or since.

No dramatic soprano has quite been up to the part since Callas so the spotlight has focussed instead on the almost equally difficult tenor role of Enzo Grimaldo, sung by Di Stefano in 1956, Bergonzi in 1963 and 1973 and Pavarotti in 1980. The latest *Gioconda* too was a perfect example of how the Arena can still breathe life into an opera that is now all but ignored by other Italian opera houses. Plenty of enthusiasm still for the famous arias and guaranteed acclaim for the *Dance of the hours*, the only surviving scrap of the Italian ballet repertoire of the 1800s.

CARMEN
1 9 8 4

Carmen	GAIL GILMORE
Don José	JOSÉ CARRERAS
Escamillo	GARBIS BOYAGIAN
Micaëla	MIETTA SIGHELE
Dancaire	GIANNI DE ANGELIS
Remendado	FLORINDO ANDREOLLI
Zuniga	CARLO DEL BOSCO
Morales	ORAZIO MORI
Conductor	GIUSEPPE PATANÉ
Producer	MAURO BOLOGNINI
Scenery	PAOLO BREGNI
Choreography	GIUSEPPE CARBONE
Costumes	LUISA SPINATELLI
Chorus master	TULLIO BONI

The Arena's 1984 Carmen was memorable not only for the production and scenery but also for Gail Gilmore's fiery Carmen (left) and José Carreras's rounded portrait of his namesake. Other productions of Bizet's opera at the Arena have been sung by even better voices, but with Bolognini's production and the cinegenic physique of the two stars complementing their musical talents the conditions were right for ideal realizations of the popular heroes of Prosper Merimée's story.

CARMEN
1 9 9 0

Carmen	GRACE BUMBRY
Don José	VERIANO LUCHETTI
Escamillo	GIORGIO ZANCANARO
Micaëla	ALIDA FERRARINI
Dancaire	GIUSEPPE RIVA
Remendado	PIERO DE PALMA
Zuniga	JACQUES MARS
Morales	SERGIO BENSI
Conductor	DANIEL NAZARETH
Producer	JACQUES KARPÒ
Designer	BERROCAL
Choreography	EL CAMBORIO
Chorus master	ALDO DANIELI

The 1990 production of Carmen *is remembered for the convincingly Spanish atmosphere created by Berrocal's scenery and for the dancing of the El Camborio company with prima ballerina Lucia Real. Controversial but interesting the scenery, which incorporated Berrocal's own wooden sculptures, and wild enthusiasm for the dancers in Act II and before the bullfight in Act IV.*

Carmen	GIOVANNA CASOLLA
Don José	NEIL SHICOFF
Escamillo	GIORGIO ZANCANARO
Micaëla	ALIDA FERRARINI
Dancaire	ANDREA SNARSKY
Remendado	MARIO BOLOGNESI
Zuniga	ARMANDO CAFORIO
Morales	ANDREA PICCINNI
Conductor	VYEKOSLAV SUTEY
Producer	ANTOINE BOURSEILLER
Scenery	RINALDO OLIVIERI
Costumes	ROSALIE VARDA
Choreography	JEREMY LESLIE-SPINKS
Chorus master	ARMANDO TASSO

The 1993 Carmen *is destined to be remembered chiefly for the unusual exclusion of the dance scenes and for the inclusion of anachronistic contemporary elements. Sterling performances from the singers, especially from Giovanna Casolla (seen below) and tenor Neil Shicoff, though he cannot have been helped by a costume suggesting a library clerk rather than a dragoon in the Alcalà.*

CARMEN
1 9 9 3

ANDREA CHENIER
1986

Andrea Chénier	José Carreras
Carlo Gerard	Renato Bruson
Maddalena	Montserrat Caballé
Bersi	Laura Zannini
Countess	Mirella Caponetti
Madelon	Jone Jori
Pierre Fléville	Giuseppe Riva
Conductor	Gianluigi Gelmetti
Producer	Attilio Colonnello
Designer	Attilio Colonnello
Choreography	Enzo Carbone
Chorus master	Aldo Danieli

With Giordano's Andrea Chénier, *the Arena made a gallant attempt to live up to past traditions and assemble a cast of the world's finest singers, including* Montserrat Caballé *(seen below with Mirella Caponetti), Carreras and Bruson. If the result was less than overwhelming it was because not all singers with exceptional voices have acting talents to match.*

ANDREA CHENIER
1 9 8 6

ANDREA CHENIER
1 9 8 6

Scenery, costumes and production were all by Attilio Colonnello. The idea of recreating the grounds of Versailles in the Arena, waterworks and and all, is an exciting one in itself, but out of place for an opera like Andrea Chénier, *which requires more intimate surroundings for a story based more on human interaction than heroic events.*

Left, José Carreras, and below, Osvaldo Di Credico and Orazio Mori.

LA GIOCONDA
1 9 8 8

La Gioconda	Giovanna Casolla
Laura Adorno	Bruna Baglioni
Alvise Badoero	Bonaldo Giaiotti
La cieca	Viorica Cortez
Enzo Grimaldo	Bruno Beccaria
Barnaba	Silvano Carroli
Zuàne	Ezio Maria Tisi
Conductor	Christian Badea
Producer	Jean-Claude Auvray
Scenery	Mario Garbuglia
Choreography	Mario Pistoni
Costumes	Jacob Jost
Chorus master	Aldo Danieli

Designers these days tend to suggest rather than slavishly obey the instructions given by the librettist of Ponchielli's La Gioconda. *In 1988 Mario Garbuglia invented his own Venice, with various monuments and ordinary houses and even the Bucintoro. The richly elaborate costumes were designed by Jacob Jost.*

LA GIOCONDA
1988

CAVALLERIA RUSTICANA
1 9 8 9

Santuzza	FIORENZA COSSOTTO
Lola	ANNA DI MAURO
Turiddu	NICOLA MARTINUCCI
Alfio	SILVANO CARROLI
Lucia	SERENA PASQUALINI
Conductor	NELLO SANTI
Producer	FLAVIO TREVISAN
Designer	FERRUCCIO VILLAGROSSI
Chorus master	ALDO DANIELI

The traditional way of designing Mascagni's Cavalleria rusticana *for the Arena is to range its Sicilian village setting on the rocky "mountainside" of the curve behind the stage. Ferruccio Villagrossi followed the convention for his 1989* Cavalleria *and made a feature of the "Arena" arch, which is also so typical of the towns of Magna Graecia. An unusual (for the Arena) aspect of this production of the archetypal Italian* verismo *opera was the fact that every member of the cast was Italian.*

Below, Anna Di Mauro as Lola.

CAVALLERIA RUSTICANA

Santuzza	GHENA DIMITROVA
Lola	ANNA SCHIATTI
Turiddu	KRISTIAN JOHANNSSON
Alfio	PAOLO GAVANELLI
Lucia	LAURA ZANNINI
Conductor	YURI AHRONOVITCH
Producer	GABRIELE LAVIA
Designer	GIOVANNI AGOSTINUCCI
Chorus master	ARMANDO TASSO

Traditionally, Cavalleria Rusticana *at the Arena is presented in tandem with a ballet or another one-act opera, often Leoncavallo's* I pagliacci. *In Verona in 1993, Gabriele Lavia's controversial but intelligent production used a single set for both the operas. Designer Giovanni Agostinucci changed just a few details to distinguish between their respective Sicilian and Calabrian settings.*

Nedda	CECILIA GASDIA
Canio	PLACIDO DOMINGO
Tonio	LEO NUCCI
Peppe	FRANCESCO PICCOLI
Silvio	ANTONIO SALVADORI
Conductor	YURI AHRONOVITCH
Producer	GABRIELE LAVIA
Designer	GIOVANNI AGOSTINUCCI
Chorus master	ARMANDO TASSO

All the action took place on a single large platform, as often happens in contemporary drama productions.

Left, Leo Nucci as Tonio.

Below, Antonio Salvadori and Cecilia Gasdia.

Opposite, Leo Nucci and Placido Domingo.

NORMA
1994

Norma	MARIA DRAGONI
Pollione	CHRIS MERRITT
Oroveso	CARLO COLOMBARA
Adalgisa	MARTINE DU PUY
Clotilde	MANUELA CUSTER
Flavio	ALDO BOTTION
Conductor	GUSTAV KUHN
Producer	WERNER HERZOG
Scenery	MAURIZIO BALÒ
Costumes	FRANZ BLUMAUER
Lighting design	VINICIO CHELI
Chorus master	ARMANDO TASSO

*The 1994 production of
Vincenzo Bellini's* Norma
*suffered somewhat by
comparison with the memory
of other performances of the
opera at the Arena. There
was criticism of the singers
(though the international
opera scene these days offers
few artists of the necessary
calibre) and even more of
designer Maurizio Balò's
lava flow laid down the side
of the amphitheatre and
glowing fiery red at the end
of the opera. Martine Du Puy
sang an impeccable
Adalgisa.*

THE ARENA
AND BALLET

Remo Schiavo

THE STARS OF THE DANCE WORLD

A short introduction is needed if we are to understand the logic underlying the history of ballet at the Arena, from its uncertain beginnings to its present flourishing state. When *Aida* was produced for the first time in the amphitheatre, in 1913, Italian dance was at its nadir, the butt of merciliess sarcasm on the part of Diaghilev. Its stars were scattered all over the world, choreographers were bereft of inspiration and the corps de ballet of a theatre like La Scala was reduced to providing supporting interludes for operas or overblown performances of choreographed mime of the type devised by Manzotti-Marenco. Just as we now wonder at the approximate and tasteless performances of the great singers of the 1800s, so dance was little but the empty repetition of hackneyed steps and routines in the ballets that inexorably followed every opera. Ballet entered the Arena in any case with *Aida*, which has three ballet sequences, and it also featured in *Carmen*, *Il figliol prodigo*, *Samson et Dalila* and other operas. With more or less randomly selected troupes of dancers and a single soloist, ballet was always an element of secondary importance in the structure of any performance. Ballet proper made its first appearance in the Arena in 1924 with *Il carillon magico*, with music by Riccardo Pick Mangiagalli and choreography by Maria and Ezio Cellini. Prima ballerina was the glamorous Lia Fornaroli, star of La Scala under Toscanini and a favourite dancer of Enrico Cecchetti, the legendary ballet master of the Imperial Russian Ballet. To find a programme containing another independent ballet we have to wait until 1935 and *Scheherazade*, presented to fill out the evening beside *Cavalleria rusticana*. Boris Romanof devised the ballet to Rimsky-Korsakov's music for another star from La Scala, Bianca Gallizia. But the Arena really began to explore its potential for ballet after the War, when finally a genuine corps de ballet, again from La Scala, presented Ravel's *Bolero*, splendidly choreographed by Aurel M. Millos and with Luciana Novaro and Ugo Dell'Ara a magnificent pair of soloists. The rest of the same evening's programme featured *Coppelia*, *Invitation to the Dance*, and *The Three-cornered Hat*. This was the first time the ballet had attempted to claim a full place for itself in the opera season by stealing a whole evening from opera. In 1952 the Arena was host to the London International Ballet, with *Gaieté parisienne* accompanying *Cavalleria rusticana* and *Swan Lake* and *Sleeping Beauty* presented with all the splendour of the latter years of the Russian Empire. Undisputed star of the company was Mona Inglesby, who

enraptured the balletomanes just as Maria Callas and Nicola Rossi Lemeni enthralled the opera buffs. The corps de ballet of La Scala returned in 1954 with an eclectic programme ranging from *Les Sylphides* to *Capriccio spagnolo* and with new names Vera Colombo and Carla Fracci appearing beside those of the more established Olga Amati, Luciana Novaro and Ugo Dell'Ara. Then in 1955 Prokofiev's celebrated *Romeo and Juliet* swept into the Arena and eventually became a regular presence, almost on the same scale as *Aida*. Olga Amati and Violetta Verdy alternated in the role of Juliet, while Romeo was shared between Giulio Perugini and Mario Pistoni. Alfredo Rodriguez provided the choreography and La Scala the corps de ballet. Despite the success of *Romeo and Juliet* and the expectations of the public, ballet did not return to the Arena until 1964, but then the international stars dancing with the London Festival Ballet in *Swan Lake* drew wild acclaim from the same audience that had shortly before applauded *Cavalleria rusticana*. The *étoiles* were Galina Samptsova, Genia Melikowa, Irina Adams and Desmond Kelly and choreography was by Vaclav Orlikovski. It wasn't until 1966 that Arena audiences had the chance to see a real Russian ballet company, when the renowned Kirov Ballet of Leningrad (now once again the Maryinski Ballet of St. Petersburg) presented Constantin Sergueev version of Tchaikovsky's *Sleeping Beauty*. There was no supporting *Cavalleria* but audiences flocked to the Arena to admire and applaud the legendary dancers of the Kirov: Alla Ossipenko, Yuri Soloviev, Irina Kolpakova and Vladien Semienov. In the following year (1967) the corps de ballet of the Kiev Opera Company brought Boris Assafieff's *The Fountain of Bakhchisarai* and showed how even without international stars the Russians could put on an exotic and wholly delightful show. 1970 was the year Carla Fracci made her Arena debut as a prima ballerina, in *Giselle*. The American Ballet Theater was a first-rate company and with Ted Kivit as her Prince Albrecht in place of the scheduled Erik Bruhn, Fracci danced an acclaimed Giselle and was showered with flowers at the end. Thenceforth the name of Carla Fracci dominates the history of ballet at the Arena. She was Juliet to James Urbain's Romeo in Prokofiev's ballet, with the La Scala corps de ballet in 1971, and danced in Léo Delibes' *Coppelia* in the following year. In 1973 she appeared with Paolo Bortoluzzi in Prokofiev's *Cinderella*, produced by Beppe Menegatti, and drew record crowds for a ballet at the Arena. Then another *Giselle* in 1974, when the crowds of extras demanded by the production perhaps got in the way of the choreography. This was followed by further odd productions of the great Tchaikovsky ballet in which Carla Fracci was always the guarantee of success.

In the 1970s many of the ballet performances at the Arena were the work of Maurice Béjart and his "Ballet du XXe siècle." They made a triumphant start in 1975 with Beethoven's *Symphony no. 9* and followed up superbly in 1977 with a show Béjart himself devised for the Arena: *Golestan*, based on traditional Iranian music, *V for ...*, with extracts from Verdi operas, and finally, Ravel's *Bolero*, danced by Carla Fracci.

The last decade has seen a series of strange programmes, evidently a reflection of the confused state of the Italian dance world, wavering between classical revival and more modern forms of dance expression, in particular those being developed in America. *Excelsior* - an affectionately ironic evocation of *fin de siècle* Italy, with Progress rampant and Obscurantism all but extinct - was presented with almost unchanged casts in 1983 and 1984. With Filippo Crivelli's subtle production and scenery and costumes designed by Giulio Coltellacci, the Arena's *Excelsior* repeated the success it had enjoyed at the Maggio Musicale in Florence and at La Scala. There was plenty to smile at with the contorsions of Jacques Dombrovsky as Obscurantism struggling against Count Volta's electrical inventions, against newfangled steamboats and explosives in the Simplon Tunnel, but in the scene on the shore of the Red Sea, where the Suez Canal is being cut, there was a pas de deux with Carla Fracci as Civilization and Gheorghe Iancu as the Slave which epitomised the La Scala school before its stars all emigrated to the Imperial Theatre in St. Petersburg. When Carla Fracci returned with *Giselle* in 1985 she was still peerless in a part that might have been created for her, but Elisabetta Terabust now alternated with the diva, and Charles Jude, *étoile* of the Paris Opéra, regularly replaced Gheorghe Iancu. Algida Myrtha, queen of the Villi, was danced by Renata Calderini. For the 1987 *Nutcracker*, the Arena moved away from the Fracci-Menegatti partnership to explore exciting new talents such as Oriella Dorella, Anna Razzi and Elisabetta Terabust alternating as prima ballerina, with Patrick Dupond and Peter Schaufuss as the Prince. New faces, and new departures for ballet at the Arena. *Zorba the Greek* by M. Theodorakis enjoyed spectacular success in two seasons (1988 and 1990), while Nino Rota's *La strada* was also admired in 1989. Though

Zorba was described as a giant with the head of a dwarf - an insubstantial story based on the famous film, with a huge orchestra and the chorus by turns participating and commentating, as in a Greek tragedy - audiences adored it because of the scintillating performances of Ekaterina Maximova, Vladimir Vassilev and Gheorghe Iancu. *La strada*, with its southern setting based on the Fellini film and ideally appropriate music by Nino Rota, proved an excellent choice of partner for yet another *Cavalleria rusticana* in 1989. The gentle and extremely moving Carla Fracci made her own the part played in the film by the unforgettable Giulietta Masina, and her Zampanò was the excellent Mario Pistoni, who also devised the choreography. The more recent ballet performances at the Arena bring us, all too late, to Rudolf Nureyev. He never in fact danced at the Arena when at the height of his fame and in full possession of his formidable physical strength. When he came with the Minkus *Don Quixote* in 1981 he was but a shadow of the "Tartar" who had dazzled audiences with his stupendous acrobaticism. He was still an extraordinarily magnetic presence on stage, but every difficult step seemed to be accompanied by a grimace of pain. Fortunately his Kitri was the splendid Eva Evdokimova so the triumph of their pas de deux was assured. In the same season the Arena also welcomed the Cuban National Ballet, with Alicia Alonso as both director and prima ballerina. Nureyev returned to the Arena for the 1991 *Romeo and Juliet*, but only as choreographer because Gheorghe Iancu was engaged to dance Romeo with the timeless Carla Fracci. And in the end, a dispute between Nureyev and the corps de ballet, which had been smouldering since a *Death in Venice* at the Teatro Filarmonico, led also to a different choreography being chosen. Perhaps it was after all destined that the memories of the Arena's balletomanes should remain forever loyal to the *Romeo and Juliet* presented by Moscow's Bolshoi Ballet in 1982: after a performance by the Bolshoi corps de ballet any other troupe looks inadequate or unsure, and never was the amphitheatre so utterly absorbed in the story of Verona's famous young lovers as when they were danced by Alexandr Bogatyrev and Natalia Bessmerntova or Viaceslav Gordeev and Nadezda Pavlova, never so thrilled as when Michail Civin or Viktor Barykin danced Mercutio.
It is only on such truly historic occasions and for such phenomenal artists that the Arena generates its ultimate and utterly overwhelming ovations.

Left, scene from the 1990 Zorba the Greek, *with Diego Ciavatti, Gheorghe Iancu and Luciana Savignano.*

ROMEO AND JULIET
1 9 8 2

Romeo	ALEXANDER BOGATYREV
Juliet	NATALIA BESSMERTNOVA
Tybalt	ALEXSEI LAZAREV
Mercutio	MIKHAIL CIVIN
Paris	MIKHAIL GABOVIC
Nurse	AGNESSA BALIEVA
Conductor	ALGIS ZHURAITIS
Choreography	YURI GRIGOROVIC
Designer	SIMON VIRSALADZE
Corps de ballet	BOLSHOI THEATRE

One of the Arena's proudest moments came in 1982 with Prokofiev's Romeo and Juliet in a production danced by Moscow's Bolshoi Ballet. Verona has seen many other fine versions but this was certainly closer to the spirit of the composer and gave superb opportunities for the company's fine male dancers and one of the virtuoso stars of world ballet. With the aid of modern mass communications, many of the great but barely known dancers in the double company which the Bolshoi brought to Verona have since become household names.

Below, Alexei Lazarev as Tybalt.

Opposite, Alexander Bogatyrev and Natalia Bessmertnova.

ROMEO AND JULIET
1991

Juliet's father	LUDOVICO DURST
Juliet's mother	SALLY WILSON
Juliet	CARLA FRACCI
Tybalt	BRUNO MILO
Rosalind	ROSALBA GARAVELLI
Romeo's father	PAOLO DURO
Romeo's mother	ROSANNA AMBROSO
Romeo	GHEORGHE IANCU
Benvoglio	CRISTIAN CRACIUN
Mercutio	BENITO MARCELLINO
Conductor	MARKO LETONJA
Choreography	JOHN CRANKO/LORIS GAI
Producer	BEPPE MENEGATTI
Designer	LUISA SPINATELLI
Ballet director	GIUSEPPE CARBONE

Carla Fracci must be the greatest Juliet of our day. The Bolshoi ballerinas may have been technically superior but as an actress, with a face that expressed every most subtle feeling of Shakespeare's heroine, she was unrivalled.
Fracci's Romeos included James Urbain (1971) and Gheorghe Iancu (1991), seen partnering her right and opposite.

SWAN LAKE
1 9 8 2

Finally, and after many relative failures, it was realized that the only version of Swan Lake *is the Bolshoi Ballet's, successful because true to the original. Despite the excellence of Carla Fracci (left) and moderate popularity with the public, the 1982 production has never been revived at the Arena.*

Principal dancers	CARLA FRACCI
	GHEORGHE IANCU
	JONATHAN KELLY
	BRUNO VESCOVO
	VIERA MARKOVIC
	LUDWIG DURST
	AURORA BENELLI
	ANNAMARIA GROSSI
Conductor	ENRICO DE MORI
Choreography	ALFRED RODRIGUES
Producer	BEPPE MENEGATTI
Designer	LUISA SPINATELLI
Corps de ballet	ARENA DI VERONA

EXCELSIOR
1 9 8 3 - 1 9 8 4

Giulio Coltellacci's scenery for Excelsior *by Marenco made ironic reference to all the myths of late-XIX Cent. Italy which, despite the threatening undercurrent of social unrest insisted on dreaming of progress, freedom and universal peace.*
Coltellacci had originally made his designs for a production at La Scala, but with small adjustments managed to adapt them to the far bigger stage of the Arena.

GISELLE
1 9 8 5

Giselle	CARLA FRACCI
Albrecht	GHEORGHE IANCU
Hilarion	JACQUES DOMBROWSKI
Myrtha	RENATA CALDERINI
Conductor	MICHEL SASSON
Dramaturge	BEPPE MENEGATTI
Scenery	BENI MONTRESOR
Choreography	GIUSEPPE CARBONE
Costumes	MARIA LETIZIA AMADEI
Ballet director	GIUSEPPE CARBONE
Maître de ballet	KONSTANTIN DAMIANOV

Though revised by Giuseppe Carbone, Adolphe Adam's celebrated ballet Giselle *appeared faithful to the original.*
The peerless Carla Fracci is the only Giselle to have captured hearts of the Arena public since the ballet's first appearance there in 1970. Perhaps the 1985 production, like its predecessor in 1974, gave too much importance to the presence of extras, who in fact did nothing to enhance the ballet's exquisite simplicity.

Principal dancers	ORIELLA DORELLA
	PATRICK DUPOND
	ROSALBA GARAVELLI
	CRISTIAN CRACIUN
	LUISA BENEDINI
	LINO CIGALA
	CELSO DE ALMEIDA
	EUGEN VADUVA
Conductor	MICHAEL COLLINS
Choreography	NICOLAS BERIOZOFF
Scenery	RAFFAELE DEL SAVIO
Costumes	MARIA LETIZIA AMADEI
Ballet director	MARIO PISTONI
Maître de ballet	ROBERT STRAJNER

1987 and Tchaikovsky's Nutcracker saw the beginning of the decline of ballet in the Arena (ballet performances have recently been transferred to the Roman Theatre). Relentlessly splendid set-piece scenery, hundreds of extras and acrobatic spectacle will never by themselves fill seats; audiences come more because Carla Fracci is dancing than because a particular ballet is billed.

This Nutcracker was remarkable for the number of first-rate dancers it assembled, including Oriella Dorella, Elisabetta Terabust, Anna Razzi (opposite, bottom left), Patrick Dupond and Peter Schaufuss.

1 9 8 8	
Zorba	VLADIMIR VASSILIEV
John	GHEORGHE IANCU
Marina	ROSALBA GARAVELLI
Yorgos	CRISTIAN CRACIUN
Conductor	MIKIS THEODORAKIS
Producer	LORCA MASSINE
Choreographer	LORCA MASSINE
Designer	FERRUCCIO VILLAGROSSI
Ballet director	PIERRE LACOTTE
Maître de ballet	GÉRARD LIGNON
Chorus master	ALDO DANIELI

1 9 9 0	
Zorba	VLADIMIR VASSILIEV
John	GHEORGHE IANCU
Marina	LUCIANA SAVIGNANO
Yorgos	DIEGO CIAVATTI
Conductor	MIKIS THEODORAKIS
Producer	LORCA MASSINE
Choreographer	LORCA MASSINE
Designer	FERRUCCIO VILLAGROSSI
Ballet director	GIUSEPPE CARBONE
Maître de ballet	LUC BOUY
Chorus master	ALDO DANIELI

Zorba the Greek *by Mikis Theodorakis is the only ballet commissioned by the Arena authority and specifically created for performance in the Arena. Its remarkable success was due to the striking scenery* by Ferruccio Villagrossi, *Lorca Massine's choreography and the music of Mikis Theodorakis, as well as magnificent performances by Vladimir Vassiliev (left) and Gheorghe Iancu.*

ZORBA THE GREEK
1 9 8 8 - 1 9 9 0

LA STRADA
1 9 8 9

Gelsomina	CARLA FRACCI
Madman	CRISTIAN CRACIUN
Zampanò	MARIO PISTONI
Conductor	ARMANDO GATTO
Choreographer	MARIO PISTONI
Scenery	FERRUCCIO VILLAGROSSI
Costumes	MARIA LETIZIA AMADEI

The delightful ballet La strada, *set to the music Nino Rota composed for the film of the same name directed by Federico Fellini, was seen first at the Teatro Filarmonico and subsequently enjoyed similar success at the Arena. Carla Fracci, an unforgettable Gelsomina, alternated in the role with Oriella Dorella (left), and Mario Pistoni gave a moving portrait of Zampanò as well as providing the sensitive and intelligent choreography.*

SPARTACUS
1 9 9 3

Spartacus	ZOLTAN SOLYMOSI
Crassus	RAFFAELE PAGANINI
Varynia	JOYCE CUOCO
Nubian	MYRNA KAMARA
African	JHANE HILL
Crixus	GIOVANNI PATTI
Choreography	YOURI VAMOS
Conductor	ROBERTO TOLOMELLI
Scenery	MICHAEL SCOTT
Ballet director	JEREMY LESLIE-SPINKS
Light Designer	HERMANN MUENZER

Anyone expecting a Spartacus à la Bolshoi (the ballet was one of the highlights of the celebrated Moscow company's tours in the West) will have been very disappointed by the production at the Arena in 1993. Choreographer Youri Vamos chose to emphasize the clash of two civilizations, the Roman and the barbarian, rather than the story of poor Spartacus, slave and then rebel gladiator. Raffaele Paganini gave a convincing performance as the cruel Crassus and Paul Boyd was an athletic and moving Spartacus.

SPARTACUS
1 9 9 3

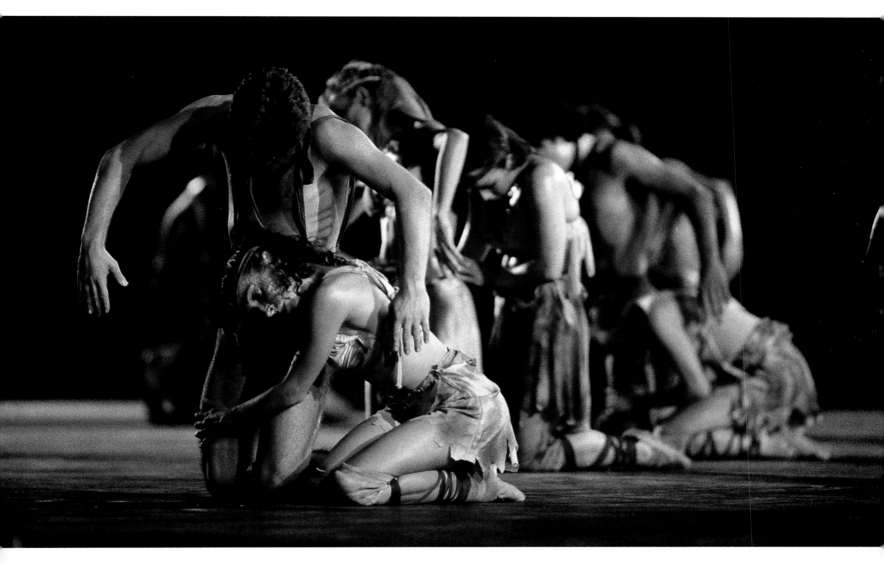

R. Pasini
R. Schiavo
THE VERONA ARENA
THE LARGEST
OPERA HOUSE
IN THE WORLD
Arsenale Editrice
(VR) 3789

Printed in July 1995
at EBS, Editoriale Bortolazzi-Stei
San Giovanni Lupatoto (Verona)